Fred Hamilton

A trip over the Intercolonial including articles on the mining industries of Nova Scotia & New Brunswick

Fred Hamilton

A trip over the Intercolonial including articles on the mining industries of Nova Scotia & New Brunswick

ISBN/EAN: 9783337148263

Printed in Europe, USA, Canada, Australia, Japan

Cover: Foto ©Andreas Hilbeck / pixelio.de

More available books at **www.hansebooks.com**

A TRIP

OVER THE INTERCOLONIAL

INCLUDING

ARTICLES ON THE MINING INDUSTRIES

OF

NOVA SCOTIA AND NEW BRUNSWICK

WITH

A DESCRIPTION OF THE CITIES OF ST. JOHN AND HALIFAX.

BY

FRED. J HAMILTON,

(Special Correspondent.)

RE-PRINTED FROM THE MONTREAL "GAZETTE."

MONTREAL :
"GAZETTE" PRINTING HOUSE, NEXT THE NEW POST OFFICE.
1876.

ENGINEERS' TOOLS.

LATHES, PLANERS, DRILLS, SHAPERS, PUNCH AND SHEARING MACHINES, &c.

STEAM ENGINES, VERTICAL AND HORIZONTAL, 10 Horse Power and upwards.

Full Specifications of all Machines will be furnished on application.

JAMES INGLIS,

327 Commissioners Street, Montreal.

THE MONTREAL
WAREHOUSING COMPANY.

SIR HUGH ALLAN, PRESIDENT.

A. W. OGILVIE, M.P.P., VICE-PRESIDENT.

MESSRS. C. J. BRYDGES.

ANDREW ALLAN.

SIR FRANCIS HINCKS.

This Company receives goods on Storage.   Property may be consigned direct to the Company or to its care.

GEO. H. HANNA,   JOHN S. HALL,
    SECRETARY.   MANAGER.

MONTREAL, September, 1876.

A TRIP

OVER

THE INTERCOLONIAL.

NO. 1.

FROM RIVIERE DU LOUP TO CACOUNA.

Owing to the short time allowed for stopping at the former place, your correspondent had no opportunity of ascertaining anything like a correct description of the starting point of the Intercolonial Railway. It is sufficiently well known, however, to the general public, and does not perhaps require any lengthy mention; except, perhaps, to add that the station arrangements were very similar to those of any other line. I tried in vain to gather a few hasty notes; but the energetic station master informed me that probably he might have an hour or so to spare in the course of a few days; but at that precise moment his hands were too full to attend to anything; adding "that the same general hurry, bustle and "business had been going on for the past two or three weeks." It may be here remarked that the business of the road is greatly facilitated by the punctual and admirable arrangements of the Grand Trunk Railway. There were no delays, no confusion among employés, or mistakes. Everything appeared to be in thorough working order, and might, so far as a stranger was concerned, have been going on precisely in the same way for the past ten years. Upon appealing to the conductor to satisfy my thirst for knowledge in the public interest, he admitted he was a comparative stranger along the road, and he could not give me any information whatever. But he was an exceedingly obliging fellow, and the way he assisted an infirm old lady to the waiting-room was the perfection of railroad gallantry. The incident was exceptional in my experience of railroad officials, and is therefore noteworthy.

Having safely deposited his charge the signal "all aboard" was given; the locomotive shrieked its loudest and we were *en route* to Cacouna, six miles distant.

We had not been aboard more than five minutes before we passed through a rock cutting some thirty or forty feet in height and about sixty yards in length, as near as could be judged. This is probably a forecast of some of the greater difficulties which have been encountered in the construction of the line at other points along the route. The road between Riviere du Loup and Cacouna is as smooth as could be wished—not even the faintest symptom of a jolt or jar. Glimpses of the Falls could here and there be obtained; but there is nothing worth mentioning in connection with the scenery, save its generally wild and varied character. Picturesque bits of rise and fall, here and there momentarily arrest the eye; but you find nothing special to fascinate your gaze until you arrive

AT CACOUNA.

Here, however, you meet your first trial, which to even a healthy man is not particularly pleasant. Four miles of muddy road, over rough rock and mire (for it had been raining heavily), seated in an apology for a carriage, the horses in which manifest a disposition to stop every five minutes, for which you cannot blame them, you finally arrive at the heart of the village. Five minutes more and the driver deposits you, considerably shaken up, at the St. Lawrence Hall.

Sixty-two in the shade, a cheerful fire and the loudest kind of ulsters I found to be the "correct thing" at this, one of the most delightful of watering-places. What a transition from the comparatively tropical region of Montreal! Here, at last, you find the perfection of repose. Fatigue and want of sleep at once gave way to admiration of the beautiful scenery from the balconies of the hotel. Perhaps it was the more welcome because the least expected. For the first time you discover that Cacouna is situated on a plateau sloping in a gradual decline to the shore of the St. Lawrence, on the south bank of which it is built. But admiration must wait upon appetite. After an excellent dinner and plenty of it—to which every one appeared to do ample justice, my kind host volunteered his services as guide, and proceeded to unfold the attractions of this charming spot. Looking due north you have an uninterrupted view for many miles. Immediately in front the bold range of the Eboulements fringes the circuit of country lying east and west. Between the river and the distant hills the sun shone upon the ascending banks of show-white fog, gilding their outlines and giving them the appearance of gilt-tipped masses of snowy vapour, while the surface of the river, gently agitated by the rippling current, sparkled in the summer light. The air was sharp and bracing. This glorious view, however, conceals the dangerous Cacouna reefs, and woe to the unfortunate, inexperienced oarsman should he venture too near them. To the north-east you have Cacouna, or Red Island, and following the same direction Green Island is noticeable for its effective and bold outline. The mouth of the Saguenay is also clearly discernable, while above this beautiful scene the purple sky streaked with bright, warm colors, gives a contrast to the whole which is almost unsurpassed for its general effect. No wonder, then, that this is such a favorite retreat for tourists from all parts of the continent. Since the opening of the line its charms have attracted a number of New Brunswickers, who were heretofore strangers to its beauties. The pleasant smell of the salt air invigorates and makes one long for a dip in the river. The usual bathing hour is when the tide comes in. The coldness of the water does not seem to deter the ladies and gentlemen from thoroughly enjoying themselves in the element. Every facility is afforded by the hotel company for this means of recreation. I should think that Cacouna is the last place in the world where a graduate of medicine would think of starting a practice. Nature has the monopoly in this respect, and judging from the sun-burnt, healthy faces of its residents, one would suppose that disease in any form was here unknown.

But Cacouna does not entirely depend upon its scenery for its popularity, for besides its scenic attractions it is a sportsman's paradise. Wild duck, wild geese, wild swan, sea duck, wigeon and teal are waiting to be shot for the amusement of the male sex. They are to be found plentifully in the vicinity of what are known as the "Brandy Pots." How the name originated is a geographical mystery; but it is probably a satire upon the fact that spirits are not allowed to be sold under the laws of the municipality of Cacouna in less quantities than three gallons at a time. The season for shooting is between the 15th of May and 1st September; but the Government does not allow the birds to be shot except as articles of food, and those who are found selling or bartering them for profit, do so at the risk of a heavy penalty. Neither is shooting allowed one hour before sunrise or one hour after sunset.

Those who may have a fondness for trout fishing can gratify it to their hearts' content. Indeed Cacouna seems to be peculiarly favored in all that pertains to watering places generally, while in many respects it is far superior.

A word with regard to the hotel. It has comfortable accommodation for 300 persons. Indeed I believe it has that number at present on its books. The rooms are large and comfortable, and if the cooking which came under my personal attention is a fair sample of its average quality, it ought to satisfy the most fastidious dyspeptic. The grounds are large and well arranged, with every conceivable convenience for juvenile sports. There is a cricket ground, archery, boating house, "merry go round," bathing-house, swings, croquet lawns, yachts, bowling alleys, billiards, and in short everything any reasonable person could desire, at a moderate cost. The view from any part of the establishment is a picture. The servants attached to the place are attentive and know their business.

In addition to the St. Lawrence Hall there are a number of smaller hotels and summer residences, some of them perfect gems in their way, extending for four miles along the plateau. Among the more prominent on the Cacouna Road is the seat of Sir Hugh Allan, a large square stone building in the midst of spacious lawn, garden, shrubbery and woodland, comprising about thirteen acres. On the opposite side is the summer cottage of Mr.

Joseph Hickson, with grounds attached. It is a neat unpretentious, home-like villa, apparently intended for comfort as well as ornament. At the commencement of the village coming from Riviere du Loup you pass the well-known seat of the Hon. James Ferrier. Adjoining the hotel, Mr. Andrew Allan's elegant cottage stands out prominent and picturesque. Next to it Mr. H. M. Gault of the Exchange Bank owns a property formerly occupied by Mr. Mackenzie. Close by is the summer retreat of Mr. Freer, the former Postmaster of Montreal. The varied architecture of the private residences, most of which are painted white, considerably adds to the natural beauty of Cacouna, their most striking feature being the general air of thorough comfort.

The spiritual wants of the people are provided for by the Anglican, Roman Catholic and Presbyterian Churches—neat edifices, the largest of which is the Roman Catholic.

The population proper, not including summer visitors, of Cacouna, numbers some 2,000 persons. It mainly consists of farmers, who seem only to to care about raising sufficient for their own consumption. The supplies for the hotels come from Montreal and Quebec. The people seem to be easy, good-natured and contented ; but ask any of them a question (at least such was my experience) and they'll invariably respond, " don't know."

The parish covers an area of some seven miles, and in the course of a long walk in which I interviewed from fifteen to twenty persons with some enquiry touching local matters, the only individual in whom I succeeded in awakening an interest was an Indian, who wanted to negociate for bead baskets at a dollar each, which I could buy in Montreal for half the money. Finding his endeavors unsuccessful, he finally was reduced to the same level as his white brother, and like him " didn't know." I am much afraid that these simple people's education has been sadly neglected in that mad pursuit for wealth, characteristic of places of a larger growth. However, as I did'nt care about purchasing intelligence at the cost of my pocket, I gave up the further pursuit of knowledge respecting this really charming spot.

No. II.

FROM CACOUNA TO TROIS PISTOLES.

Returning from the village of Cacouna to the station, during which the horses travelled at a rate of speed only attained once a month, so the driver informed me, I found the train was an hour late. I fully believe that had those horses been aware of the fact they would have walked all the way. Having plenty of time on my hands, I took a turn around the outskirts of some of the farms along the railroad track. In almost every instance ignorance and neglect on the part of their owners seemed to pervade those apologies for fields, enclosed by abject apologies for fences. Good, rich land, most of it black loam, was given over to the weeds. It is true there

had been an attempt made to clean a few fields, probably several decades
since, and the effort was evidently one worth commemorating; for to mark
the spots when these feats of industry had been achieved, piles of stones
lie in the centre of the fields, moss-grown and covered with bankrupt verdure. Seriously speaking, the *habitants* of Cacouna do not appreciate the
wealth which Nature has given them. Probably the advantages of the
Intercolonial may dawn upon their imaginations say thirty or forty years
from now; but judging from the present indication I am afraid my antici-
pations are a trifle premature.

At 2 o'clock the train arrived in sight, and after many efforts stopped
about five hundred yards *above* the station, another illustration of the
proverb "The more haste, the less speed." This, I afterwards ascertained
from the conductor, was owing to an accident to the patent air brakes; two
of the tubes of which had burst, thereby rendering the vacuums partly
inoperative. The same official said he had patched them up as well as he
could, but had some of the more nervous passengees been aware that they
had travelled with broken air brakes below them, I fancy they would have
been somewhat anxious. Of course the mishap was unforseen, but the
incident should be mentioned. Trifles such as these sometimes give birth
to "Appalling Accidents" and "Coroner's Inquests."

ST. ARSENE

is the next stopping place on the road, four miles distant from Cacouna.
Between the two the grade is very steep, although the cuttings through
which the track passes are not deep. The sub-soil is mostly rock, with a
surface soil of clay and loam. The village lies south of Cacouna and has
a population of about two thousand souls. The land is remarkably rich,
consisting of red clay and loam. The population is exclusively agricultural,
and the farms in this small place are said to be excelled by none in the
Province for richness and average yield of acreage. To show you how
greatly in advance are these people of their neighbors in Cacouna, it was
stated to me, and not by a resident, that many of the farmers are worth
$20,000 a piece, most of which has been derived from the receipt of agri-
cultural produce. Eight miles east of St. Arsene is

ISLE VERTE,

having a population of four thousand persons. It is in the county and
district of Temiscouata. On the island itself, from which the parish takes
its name, there are about 60 farmers, who subsist chiefly on agriculture and
fishing. My informant, an intelligent gentleman, residing at Trois Pistoles,
and who has travelled extensively on this continent and in England,
assured me that the shooting at this place is unsurpassed. In the spring
and fall there are thousands of wild geese, ducks, snipe and larks. In fact
the island is said to literally swarm with them at these seasons of the year.
The fishery, too, is said to be the best between Quebec and Rimouski.
Herring, sardines, shad, eels, and a few salmon are the staple articles of
pisciculture. The island is comparatively unknown, although of late

years a few have visited the place for the sake of its shooting. The view from the island commands several prominent points of interest along the St. Lawrence ; but it would be invidious to name this as specially attractive, for as far as I have yet proceeded the scenery along the route has been extremely fine, almost from any point you may wish to name. The parish of Isle Verte is located on the main land, opposite the island. The greater part of it lies low, beneath the hill which faces the river. The people are exclusively French, and are, of course, Roman Catholics. There is a church and twelve schools, and the inhabitants are moral, thrifty and attend to their own business. Ten miles further east you arrive at

TROIS PISTOLES,

which is a place of some importance. As you approach the village by the Intercolonial Railway bridge you have, from the cars, an exceedingly pleasant view of hill and dale, skirting the little river of that name, which empties itself into the St. Lawrence.

This bridge crosses the river of Trois Pistoles, and is built of iron. It is so firmly built that you cannot tell, save by the hollow murmur of the water below, that you are not on *terra firma*. Its length is five hundred feet, the height from the water to the floor being 60 feet. There is a side space for foot passengers, and the whole is a massive structure, but by no means heavy in appearance.

Before giving you a descripton of the place I must say something about

THE RAILWAY STATIONS,

which so far, are admirably built, and well adapted for the purposes required. But strange to say, the station masters don't appear to be able to give you much information respecting the resources of the country, and, in consequence you are compelled to resort to the inhabitants for details. The same smooth, easy running is maintained all along the track. What few cuttings you have to pass through are excellent specimens of excavation, the quality of the work being apparent to the most unskilled amateur in railroad engineering.

THE STATION

here bears evidence of the enterprise of the residents. Already several new buildings are in course of erection, one of which is intended as a first-class hotel ; the others will be fitted up as storehouses. A refreshment room is in operation, and is well patronised.

TROIS PISTOLES HAS A TRADITION

which dates back two hundred years ago, and from which it derives its name. I was looking for the recital of some sanguinary deed of Indian warfare, and took out my note book to record some horrible disaster in connection with the legend, which would combine romance with adventure, and "hair breadth 'scapes" from Indian torture of by-gone times, but I was mistaken, I would require a far more prolific imagination than I possess to build a novel upon the following: It is said that 200 years ago a weary, way-worn traveller was desirous of being conveyed to the opposite shore of the St. Lawrence. But the ferry man of those times refused to row him over in his gondola unless he paid him three pistoles, cash in advance. The pilgrim was about to accede to the boatman's request and pulled out the money to gratify the boatman's greed for gain, and just as he was about to hand it to that avaricious individual he dropped it in the water—and it was lost. Here the tradition ends abruptly and disappointingly. I thought it possible that some *habitant* might be able to tell me whether the traveller's ghost was looking for it yet. *That* fact would have put an interesting climax to the otherwise defective legend. But no, nobody would satisfy me with absolute certainty on this point, so I was fain to search elsewhere for facts more realistic.

THE VILLAGE

is built upon an elevation of about 60 feet above the river. The site is an excellent one for a watering place. The open river in front is very broad here, and the view when the morning tide comes in is extremely beautiful. The shore on the opposite side is flat, but the breeze is invigorating and sweet. One of the inhabitants kindly gave me several interesting facts in connection with the place. The parish is nine miles long and six miles wide. It is bounded by the St. Lawrence on the north ; on the south by what is known as the fourth range ; St. John de Dieu and Isle Verte on the west and St. Simon on the east. The population is 4,500. There is a long range of hills sheltering the village from the autumnal winds on the south, which extends a distance of six miles. At the western extremity you have the Basque Island, and at the eastern, the Islets D'Armour, two in number, but very important to the prosperity of the place. These are simply small fishing grounds. The municipality comprises a Mayor and six Councilmen.

A VERY STRICT PROHIBITORY LAW

is said to exist here ; but, like most measures of the kind, it is more honoured in the breach than in the observance. A fine of $50 is the penalty for selling whiskey without a license, for *every offence,* and as there are no licenses granted, the law becomes arbitrary. At a place where I had the honour of being an invited guest, the landlord was so overjoyed to meet a Montreal man, whom he evidently regarded as a curiosity, that he persuaded some one else to order in liquid refreshments. If the by-law regarding the sale of liquor is strictly carried out in Trois Pistoles, that landlord will have to pay $200 at the next Sessions. Just fifty dollars a piece for four drinks.

The agricultural features of this beautiful and thriving village are potatoes, rye, oats, wheat and the raising of cattle. A large number of pigs are also sold here annually. The average yield per acre of the above crops is as follows :—Potatoes, 250 bushels ; rye, 10 to 12 bushels ; oats, 25 bushels. The butter is really splendid, and finds a ready sale at 20 cents in the Quebec market. Some of the crops are a little backward, but in promising condition. Particular attention has been paid of late years to the wheat, which is said to be improving in value every year. It is expected the hay-yield will be very large, the average crop of which, heretofore, has been 2,500 lbs to the acre ; although as much as 3,000 have been reached. The soil is very rich, and, the inhabitants are fully alive to the importance which the Intercolonial Railway will be to the place. **The farms are nearly all owned by the people who till them, very few are rented.** They vary in size from 75 to 200 acres. Close by the station there is a saw mill supplied with logs from the vicinity of Lake Temiscouata, 30 miles south of the river. They are mostly spruce ; the supply of pine timber being almost exhausted. The mill gives employment to 60 persons, and was owned by Mr. G. B. Hall of Quebec. Last year two English vessels of 500 tons each were laden with timber from this point. In addition to this there are two flour mills in the village.

With reference to the commercial depression existing all over the country, its effect here has been noticeable in

THE EXTENSION OF THE CREDIT SYSTEM

to those farmers who cannot pay cash. In speaking upon the matter to an intelligent merchant he said, "that a cash business was equivalent to no business at all : you must either sell for produce, give credit, or—close up. My opinion with regard to the Intercolonial railway is that it cannot fail to benefit us ; the freights are moderate and have been lately reduced, but I cannot tell you what the scale is just now. But they are very moderate to suit the times." Upon asking another farmer about the credit system and its effect upon the people, he at first declined to give me any information. He simply said :—" You be from de Commaircial—vot you call him ?—de commaircial agenzee peeples ?" I soon set his mind at rest and finding he had a grievance, even in this peaceful spot, he eased his mind by explaining after much trouble, what oppressed him. In effect he said as follows :—" Not being able to pay cash we sell our produce and stock at a loss to ourselves, but a very large profit to the merchant, in exchange for goods. He, in his turn, sends it by the railroad to Quebec, and receives cash, while we have to content ourselves with what we get from the store." Seeing no remedy for this state of things, I sympathised with him, whereupon he sorely tempted a law-abiding citizen to score up 20 cents on the slate (another instance of the credit system) in exchange for rye ; but the tempted one stood firm and resisted the overture in view of the fifty-dollar penalty. Had that transaction been based upon a cash principle, I cannot say what might have occurred.

Besides the small fishing grounds, already referred to, there are

THREE FINE LAKES

here, which yield, during the season, a good supply of salmon, sturgeon, eels, sardines, &c. These lakes are St. Simon, east of the village, four and a half miles in length and one and a half in width ; Caron Lake lies to the south ; it is one and a half mile long, and a quarter of a mile wide ; D'Armour Lake east of Caron, is about the same area, and its trout are said to be unexcelled. In the neighborhood of the village there are 14 fisheries in all.

THE EDUCATIONAL FACILITIES,

secular and religious, are exceedingly good, among which the Convent of Jesus and Marie ranks first. It is under the control of six sisters, who attend to the education of sixty children. I was sorry my time would not allow of a personal visit. There are besides one model school, where French and English are taught, and thirteen elementary schools, exclusively French. There are also two churches, built in 1841-43. There is only one Protestant family in the village.

I am informed the older people, who are the lineal decendants of families from old France, are very illiterate, the majority of them not being able to read or write. Notwithstanding this fact, my informant tells me, they speak the language far more purely than you would suppose. The children are healthy, intelligent-looking youngsters, and are compelled to attend school regularly.

THE CRIMINAL BUSINESS

is transacted by a magistrate and three commissioners, who hold quarterly session. The transfer of deeds, &c., gives a remunerative employment to three notaries, while one barrister has his hands full in the exercise of his profession. The health of the people, as may be supposed, is good. Contagion is unknown, and only think of it ye dwellers in cities, mosquitoes and flies are strangers to the place. There are three doctors to attend to the sick of the village—when there are any to attend to. The roads are good, the water is pure, the bathing is all that could be desired, and, altogether the inhabitants of Trois Pistoles are a quiet, moral, thrifty and scrupulously clean people. The hotel accommodation is limited to two boarding houses ; but I venture to assert it will contrast favorably with any you will find at home. The boarding-house people here are not yet initiated into the mysteries of that profession, for when I enquired, by way of experiment, for hash, the matron looked as if I was propounding a conun-drum.

No. III.

FROM TROIS PISTOLES TO BIC.

In my last letter I should have mentioned in addition to the iron bridge at Riviere Du Loup (which is 300 feet long and 20 feet above the water) there is also one, half a mile west of the station of Isle Verte, of two spans of 80 feet each, of the Howe truss pattern. These, with the bridge at Trois Pistoles, already noticed, complete the number of bridges so far reached. Before leaving Trois Pistoles reference should be made to

AN ENORMOUS CUTTING OF TOUGH BLUE CLAY,

which is about a quarter of a mile from the bridge. An official of the road informed me that they had experienced more trouble with this cutting than with any other along the line. There were 200 men at work when I was there: filling in gaps made by the falling earth, and otherwise strengthening the work. There is also a side cutting on the west side 50 feet deep, and a through cutting on the east side 28 feet deep. The great difficulties which were originally encountered here were of the most disheartening character; but engineering skill has finally conquered Nature—provided Nature does not take it into her head some fine day to scatter the track with huge fragments of her handiwork. Frequent apprehensions of some such event have been expressed in my hearing by officials and passengers. There has been much discussion with reference to the wisdom of this cutting in the first place. An eminent American engineer, a member of the firm of Messrs. Clarke, Reeves & Co., of Philadelphia., contractors of two or three of the bridges along the line, which will be referred to in their proper places, is of opinion this cutting should never have been made. Of course, in the absence of a map to enable your readers to understand the topography of this part of the road, it is somewhat difficult to describe it intelligently. But I will endeavour to give you the best description I can. The cutting to the railway bridge of Trois Pistoles is in a straight line, as near as may be. The contention is that, had a curved track been made touching Tetu's Mills, a distance of about one-third of a mile south of the present track, continuing in the arc of a circle until the curve reached the continuation of the line, this enormous amount of work would have been avoided, and the cutting need never have been made. The additional length of this curve would not have been more than half a mile, and the saving to the country it is estimated, would have been one-third less. The distance from Riviere du Loup to Trois Pistoles is 27 miles.

Nine miles further we reach the village of

ST. SIMON.

The station is situated on an elevation of 292 feet above the sea level. Between Trois Pistoles and St. Simon the work along the line is very light, and does not need any special mention, except to note the same easy grade, which makes travelling a perfect luxury compared to some railway lines in the United States. The cars are comfortable and spacious, and remarkable for their elegant and thorough workmanship, although the lighting might be improved upon.

St. Simon has a population of about 700 persons. It is pleasantly located in a valley, and its chief products are hay and grain. From this point the scenery changes gradually in its character and becomes wild and rugged. As it was impossible to get off at every station, for want of time, I cannot give you more than a general idea of the surrounding view. Its principal feature is the lake of St. Simon, already referred to in my last paper, where some fine fishing may be had. Several grains of salt should be taken before arriving at any definite conclusions of the natural wealth of these small villages for the *habitants* would have you believe theirs is, of all places in the universe, the best. There are several charming bits of river and hill, but by comparison with others more noteworthy they become almost common-place.

One mile west of the next station you strike

THE FIRST SNOW SHED

after leaving **Riviere du Loup. This is cut through** 600 feet of solid rock and is 28 feet deep. **A general description of this shed will** answer for all. The roof **is flat and** is supported by "struts," or sticks at an incline, strongly secured in **the rock work.**

There is a conflict of opinion relative to the roofs. Those who profess to know say they will be almost useless in the winter time, and if they had been steep they would have been much better adapted for the purpose. The sheds appear to be very thinly roofed, although there is no doubt **that** they are well supported by hundreds of these " struts " projecting from **the** rock, each of which I should say is between three or four inches **thick.** Whether a flat roof will dislodge snow sooner than a steep one remains to be seen ; but the argument in favor of the adoption of the former **is that** the wind will have a greater sweep over a level surface than over an inclined plane. However, experience will decide the question. The next station is

ST FABIAN,

ten miles from St. Simon. Its elevation above the sea level **is 439 feet.** This is the highest point between Riviere du Loup and St. Flavie, 28 miles east of here, which will be noticed in its proper place. (It should be understood that the term " east " is used for the sake of convenience, in order to avoid the frequent changes and diversions of the line, which in reality runs between Riviere du Loup and Moncton, according to the official **time** table, from south to north. The word " east," therefore, means east of Riviere du Loup).

The population of **St.** Fabian is about **400, and it** lies south of the track. **It is also a hay and grain** country, and **possesses** exceedingly rich soil, **although but a comparatively small portion of it is** level. The crops are **in fair condition, but the heavy rains of the** past few days will not be favorable **to their advancement. A chain of lakes,** four or five in number, runs through **this portion of country,** the largest being named after the village. The **scenery here** becomes more imposing and wild ; reminding those who **have visited the** northern counties of England, of Westmoreland and Cumberland ; **as** you proceed you find **the air** becoming more chilly and bracing. One would almost fancy that the fall had arrived, and if you do not provide yourself with a **good,** warm wrapper you will be apt to repent you of your forgetfulness as the night advances. The purple hue of **the** mountains which disappear in the mist of foggy clouds has a peculiar **effect** upon the cold, grey surface **of the** water ; but **there** is a silent grandeur about the scenery, the **sombre tints of** which **are relieved** by the emerald verdure of spruce forest skirting the base of the mountains, which cannot but impress the tourist of the wonderful victory that man has achieved in this vast but solitary region. Had I the skill of those versatile authors of the dime novel series, what could I desire more than to create some glowing fiction of Indian life in the middle ages? But, alas, there are no Indians here; no, not even a bear to remind you of hunting expeditions, or of hostile invasions of hungry and famished bruins among the wigwams of the noble red men of the forest. Both Indian and bear are far more sensible, and seek their meat where they will be more likely to get it, than in this rough and almost forsaken spot. But stern realities, not imaginings, demand attention just now.

A quarter mile west of St. Fabian station you pass through another extensive snow shed, 900 feet long and 33 feet deep. This huge rock formation has cost a small fortune to excavate. It is said dislodgments frequently occur; but these slides are not serious, and a man at each section is kept busy in seeing the line is clear, a sufficient time before the arrival of each train to permit of the removal of the broken masses. This excavation is cut through a curve at a radius of 1,400 feet to the circle.

One and a half mile east of St. Fabian station an iron bridge is constructed over the Grand Bic River. This bridge is a single span of 80 feet in length and its height is 35 feet from the water.

Maintaining the same easy motion you continue onward, little dreaming of the

MAGNIFICENT SPECTACLE.

awaiting your admiration. It would not be fair to the reader to keep her or him in suspense, notwithstanding what Mr. Martin F. Tupper has to say about the sweet enjoyment of anticipation.

Two miles from Bic Station you arrive at Bic Mountain, which rises from its rocky foundation to a height of 700 feet above sea level. This grand natural monument cannot be described. It is covered with wild rough vegetation, and as you look upward from the platform of the car, the spruce trees edging the outer rim of its summit, strike you as a fitting coronet purposely placed there by Nature—the crowning crest of her Divine skill. It is almost perpendicular, made so in part by the cuttings for the track, which partially encircle it with its iron belt at a height of 220 feet from its base. To look up at it from below compels your admiration. To look down from it from above is suggestive of involuntary suicide—if there is such a thing. I regretted very much not having the acquaintance of the American tourist who after seeing the Niagara Falls, and being of the opinion that they were pretty fair, enquired when the next train was due for Boston. Because had I the pleasure of having him with me on Thursday last, and had he dared have insulted Nature with any similar remark touching Bic Mountain, it would have served him right to have put him off the cars in order to get up an enthusiasm some time during the next twenty-four hours. If a man is callous to this majestic piece of natural and artificial construction, he must be a dangerous individual and should be shunned by all conscientious people.

It was originally contemplated to build the road at the base of the mountain, but after the contract was awarded the intention was changed. Had the original idea been carried out it would have necessitated a "fill" of 330,000 yards of earth.

BIC·

Close to the station over the Little Bic River, is an iron lattice bridge, built by the Fairbairn Engineering Company of England. It has a single span of 110 feet. It is an excellent piece of work, built on stone piers of substantial Ashlan masonry, as indeed, are all the bridges along the line. The station is as an elevation of 75 feet above the sea level; and like all the stations thus far, is tastefully and substantially constructed.

But what can be said about Bic itself—one of the loveliest spots to be found on the continent! I am afraid there is nothing new that I can say about Bic. The ground has been gone over before; the scenery has been described more graphically than I could hope to attempt. Mr. J. M. Lemoine of Quebec, in his charming "Maple Leaves," has written about all that is worth writing concerning Bic, and I must refer the reader to his concise description of this modern Paradise, of which the beautiful Emily Montague desired to be queen in the year 1767. Its history dates from 1603, and through its various phases of political ups and downs it is as charming as ever. Events have not changed the tide of its natural loveliness. The railroad station may be said to be in the centre of the town. Its population numbers about 700 persons. Bic is located in a hollow and surrounded by everything charming and beautiful. Opposite the village are two islands connected at low water. One of these islands is named *Isle du Massacre.* The other shall be nameless, for the reason that it hasn't any name.

MASSACRE ISLAND

has a tradition; a genuine first-class horror. Not a mere visionary affair which leaves off in the middle in a state of uncertainty; but a *bona fide* tradition to this effect: About one hundred and fifty years ago, a party of Micmac Indians, on their way to Gaspe, stopped at the Island, first securing their canoes safely on shore. They passed the night in a cave situated in the centre of the island, large enough to accommodate their party, which numbered over one hundred young men. At that time the Micmacs were at variance with the Iroquois. A war party of the latter, in search of the unsuspecting Micmacs, came upon them suddenly in the night, built up faggots around the mouth of the cave and set fire to them. Only two of the unfortunate savages escaped the flames, but they were shot down by the poisoned arrows of their foes. Two years ago human bones and stone arrow heads were found in the cave. There is no reason to believe the tradition is a fiction. The legend does not savor of exaggeration, for recent events in connection with the massacre of Custer's men confirm the oft-repeated stories of Indian atrocities.

Looking seaward in fine weather you can see the north shore quite plainly, a distance of 30 miles. Two and a half miles east of Bic is Haute Bay. Nearly every variety of the picturesque can be seen from this watering place. In the spring there are hundreds of wild geese. The place is well sheltered by the Shickshock range, skirting the northshore of the St. Lawrence. **Two miles west** of Bic is Ha **Ha** Bay, famous for its pic-nics **and sea bathing.** The reader may remember **that** Bic is mentioned **in** connection with the contemplated Harbour of Refuge at Cape L'Original, north of the Isle du Massacre. No decision, however is yet reached by the Government in regard to this matter. A number of modern dwelling-houses are in course of erection. The hotel accommodation might be **better,** and is scarcely sufficient to meet the growing size of the place. There is no doubt that the Intercolonial Railway will be the means of making Bic *the* watering place of the future.

No. IV.

FROM BIC TO RIMOUSKI AND FATHER POINT.

The character of the scenery from Bic to Rimouski gets rougher and more grandly picturesque as you travel east. Lake and mountain, river, rock and forest get mixed up in every conceivable form it is possible to imagine. The solitude increases, and Nature dons her sternest garments, perfectly oblivious of the invasion of Science in her domains. The sun and cloud effects are extraordinary in their results. For instance, you will find the summit of a mountain peeping forth in a long narrow streak of bluish black between the golden lines of sunlight stretching across the sky. You cannot but admire what you suppose to be a rare phenomenon, when some one **informs** you that that long black mark is the summit of a mountain a dozen miles away. You think your informant is poking fun **at you ;** but you find this is literally correct. The eccentricities of shade **and** light are limitless. One half of the side of **a** mountain will appear dark and awesome ; the other half will be clothed with radiance. It has **been** raining heavily, and you see the arc of the rainbow broken in half a dozen places by inky black clouds. Towards evening the trees assume fantastic **shapes of all sorts of** designs. A superstitious person left alone in this country for half a day would get frightened out of his wits in less than half an hour. It would pay Dore to come here just for twenty-four hours, and he **would** get studies enough to last him a lifetime.

Rimouski station is only sixty-seven feet above sea level. Half a mile west of it you cross another iron bridge, 400 feet long (five spans of 80 feet each), 28 feet above the Rimouski river. The little break in the scenery around the station subdues that feeling of loneliness which begins to creep over you, and you breathe more freely when you find you have **not** reached the **end of civilization.**

RIMOUSKI.

The situation of the town, which lies low, is very pleasant, and over-looks the St. Lawrence at one of its grandest points. Immediately in front is St. Barnaby's Island, which extends nearly the entire length of the town proper. This island is associated with the name of Touissaint Cartier, who, after a narrow escape from death by shipwreck, made this place his home, where he devoted the remainder of his life to religious meditation. He died on the 29th January, 1767, and is buried beneath the doorway of the Catholic Church in the town. An interesting review of this remarkable man will be found in *Les Chroniques de Rimouski*, vol. I., p. 65, written by l'Abbe Chas. Guay, formerly Vicar of Rimouski Cathedral. There are two volumes published by G. P. Delisle, Quebec, edition 1873, copies of which should be had by every tourist who desires to know the history of this ancient place. The work is full of incident, romance and local interest. About thirty miles from here is Point Betsiamites, which lies on the opposite shore. It can be seen distinctly on a clear day. The view along the beach is very fine, and the surface of the river is pleasantly dotted by the white sails of the fishing craft, and, occasionally, ocean steamers. The houses are neatly and substantially built, the gardens in front being laid out with much taste. The population is about 2,000 and exclusively Roman Catholic. The people are hospitable and polite. Through the kindness of the Vicar-General, Rev. E. Langevin, I am enabled to present the reader with some information respecting

THE RELIGIOUS AND EDUCATIONAL SEMINARIES
of Rimouski.

The Bishop of the Diocese is the Right Rev. John Langevin. His jurisdiction comprises the districts of Rimouski, Gaspe, the county of Temiscouata and part of the county of Saguenay, from Riviere Pont Neuf to Belle Isle.

The cathedral is a large Gothic structure, built of stone, and opened in 1859. Its dimensions are 200 feet by 75 feet. The height of the steeple from the ground is 115 feet.

The educational institutions are situated on the main road, north of the station.

First, is the Convent of the Congregation of Notre Dame, in charge of Sister St. Laon. It is built on a hill named Mont St. Jean. The convent has a frontage of 70 feet, with two wings, east and west, each 70 x 45 feet. Last year there were 260 pupils receiving education here, varying from 7 to 18 years of age. The structure is of brick, of the modern style, with stone basement. It stands on an elevation of about 25 feet above the river, and was erected at a cost of £9,000. The education given is of the highest order, and to show the reader the exertions the Roman Catholic Church is making to give a good education to her children, the fees, including board, do not exceed at this convent the ridiculously small sum of *seventy-two dollars per year !*

The second institution is the Convent of the Sisters of Charity, situated north of the former building. It is in charge of Sister St. Pierre. Its dimensions are 60 x 45 feet. It is modern in style, and is in the form of a parallelogram. There is an addition being made to it which will double its present capacity. It provides a home for orphans and old ladies, and combines the advantages of a hospital, all free. Admission to the home is by election. The election is held by a Mother Superior and by a Council of five Sisters. There are two branches—one at Cacouna, the other at Carleton—in connection with this establishment.

The third institution is the College of St. Germain de Rimouski, under the direction of the following officers:—*President*, the Bishop of the Diocese; *Vice President*, Rev. Desire Vezina; *Prefect of Students*, Rev. J. Couture, A.M., Graduate of Laval University, with which the College is affiliated; *Director of Studies*, Rev. J. O. Simard; *Bursar*, Rev. Joseph Dumas. This College gives a classical, commercial and theological education. The building is of freestone, situated 200 feet south of the convent. The architecture is modern French. It is four storeys high. Its dimensions are 300 feet frontage, with ells of 100 x 50 feet. It has accommodation for 250 students. The entire course of study takes 11 years, and the students are admitted from 10 to 25 years of age. The fees are correspondingly low—in fact merely nominal, and include board and tuition for *eighty dollars per year*. The secular priests receive for their services as instructors from $50 to $100 per year, including board. This college is not yet finished, and when completed it will cost $150,000. Already $100,000 have been expended upon it. Last year a student from here won the Prince of Wales' Medal in Philosophy at Laval University.

In addition to the foregoing there are eight cloistered nuns, of the order of Carmelites, in retirement.

Nine young ladies of the Parish have formed a sisterhood, whose object is to teach the poor of the vicinity. They receive no pay for their services and engage themselves to this duty to their lives' end.

There is only one free school in the town, which went into operation August 1st. Eighty pupils have been registered, so far, on its books. But there are twelve schools in the parish, which extends about 10 miles, and is 3 miles wide.

THE MUNICIPALITY

consists of a Mayor and eight Councillors. The town was incorporated under an Act of the Quebec Legislature on the 5th April, 1869. A prohibitive liquor by-law is said to work well here. I, for one, can say I never saw any intoxicating beverage either for sale or in any person's keeping during my brief stay. The by-law certainly appears to be a success, compared with a similar one at Trois Pistoles. The Vicar-General informed me that a great difficulty is experienced in awakening the people of Rimouski to a sense of the natural advantage of the place, and they are slow to profit by the value which the Intercolonial Railway would be to them if they could only be aroused from their apathy and indifference. After much trouble and repeated public meetings resolutions were passed accepting the offer of a private company to erect water works here. This action was suggested by the disastrous fire at St. Johns, Quebec, and, as was the case there, so it is here—the only engine they have is out of repair.

There is one good feature about the towns-people of Rimouski, and should be mentioned :—The only lock-up in the place is tenantless.

The people are Conservative in politics, the main issues against the present Government being the Free School question and the subject of Divorce. It is a matter of public and out-spoken comment that the present representatives to the House of Commons and to the Quebec Legislature will not be returned at the next election.

A short distance from the town the Government has built a wharf, the pier to which is three-quarters of a mile long and thirty feet wide, connected by rails with the main line. A small tender has been built for landing the mails from the ocean steamers, for which purpose the wharf was constructed.

In concluding my hurried description of Rimouski I must not forget to refer to the excellent hotels with which it is provided. There are three or four in the town, which for home-like attractiveness, comfort, cleanliness, good food, excellent cooking and moderate charges, are equal to any I have yet seen.

SHIPWRECKS.

Rimouski has been the sad scene of several shipwrecks of more than ordinary interest. My time will not admit of giving you a detailed description of each; but I append a list of the most historical. The first notable storm of which there is any account took place on December 3rd 1832, when four wrecks occurred at the same time. These were the barques Mary Ann and Jane, the Mountaineer, the brig James Langton and the barque Emerald.

In June, 1837, the barque United kingdom went ashore. In October, 1840, the Prince George was wrecked in a storm, at another point the ship British Merchant shared the same fate.

In November, 1863, the J. K. L. narrowly escaped shipwreck, and after being detained on St. Barnaoy's Island was compelled to abandon a large portion of her rigging.

On the night of the first of November, 1870, the Elxtrick went to pieces during a violent tempest.

These instances are given by residents to show the alleged necessity for a harbour of refuge at Father Point.

FATHER POINT.

There is nothing which makes you take so kindly to the infirmities of human nature as a good breakfast before seven o'clock, a seat behind a horse that will trot a mile in less than three minutes through a fine country and over a capital road. In this happy state of mind, accompanied by a genial gentleman, I left Rimouski this morning *en route* to Father Point, six miles distant.

On our way we struck another tradition, and of course I had to stop and examine it. This time the legend is connected with the

MIRACULOUS CHURCH OF ST. ANNE,

two or three miles from Rimouski. The story goes that a remarkable cure was performed here a year ago. An invalid who had been praying to the Virgin, was suddenly cured of lameness. In gratitude he left his crutch as a thank-offering to *la Bonne Mere*. I stopped here, and went into the building, a plain brick edifice, built on an open common, facing the river. The only occupant was a devout worshipper, who looked as if he were in a final stage of consumption. He was on his knees praying away at a great rate and spitting tobacco-juice around freely. He and I were the only two persons about. The altar was dimly lighted, and the place exceedingly dirty. The worshipper seemed to consider my presence as an intrusion. But disregarding the look of annoyance that clouded his pallid features, I devoted myself to the discovery of that crutch. After a few minutes, on looking about me, I finally saw it suspended over the door, of what, apparently, is intended as a small, private chapel. Yes there it was, sure enough, a brand new crutch! Not a well-worn, greasy, dilapidated-looking relic. No. Nothing of the kind—simply some such a crutch as you could buy for a dollar. After such undeniable testimony as this I went away, perfectly satisfied that the tradition was all right. I admit I would have preferred interviewing the original owner of the article, but, however that was not important, so long as the crutch was there to convince one of the truth of the cure. Above the altar was a statue presented on the Feast of St. Anne (the 26th July), by the pilots of this district. (St. Anne is the patron saint of Mariners.) Above it is a miniature ship. Below it is a Latin text. On St. Anne's day there were 2,000 persons from all parts of the country who visited the church, including the lame the weak, and the aged of both sexes. I am told that the adjacent villages were completely depopulated for the time being; but I am not told that any miracles were performed on that occasion.

At Father Point there is a light house, pilot station, a meteorological observatory, a storm drum signal station, and a telegraph office of the Montreal Telegraph Company, all in one. The respective duties attached to these offices are ably performed by Mr. John McWilliams, who, although a young man, probably knows as much about the surrounding country as anyone. All the regular lines of river and ocean steamers have their pilots here. About 20 in all call at this point.

THE LIGHT HOUSE

is 60 feet above the level of the sea. It is lighted by five mammoth burners, each of which is reflected by an electro-plated copper disc 2 feet in diameter. To the east you can see St. Luce and St. Flavie. Looking west you have Barnaby's Island, Bic Island, (15 miles distant), and Rimouski wharf. Due south you have St. Annaclet. This point has also been mentioned as a harbour of refuge, in consequence of which a continual rivalry is kept up between Father Point and Bic.

This important signal station is probably the best known on the St. Lawrence River

---

No. V.

FROM RIMOUSKI TO THE METAPEDIAC, N.B.

Between these points, 123 miles distant, is the heaviest work along the line; running through wild, rugged country, magnificent in its silent grandeur; but perfectly useless from an agricultural stand point. To describe it would be to repeat what has already been written concerning Bic and Rimouski. It possesses the same diversified characteristics. It is, in short, one great stretch of natural barbaric splendor—one continuous upheaving of Nature, fed by a thousand streams.

The object of this letter is rather to show the gigantic skill which has been displayed by engineering science. The facts which are here presented will tell their story far more effectively than pages of elaborate word painting.

BETWEEN ST. LUCE AND MILL STREAM.

Between these stations there are nine stopping places, although but two of them are entitled to the name of stations.

Ste. Luce, ten miles east of Rimouski, is 167 feet above sea-level. It is a pretty place and grows a small quantity of grain and wheat.

Ste. Flavie, 8 miles east, is one of the two exceptions referred to. The station is large and convenient. This point is 246 feet above sea level. The town is on the shore, but the settlement continues nearly two miles along the line. A large brick engine house here is said to have cost $30,000. Four miles east of the station, the Metis River is crossed by an iron bridge of 4 spans of 100 feet each, built 36 feet above the water. Close to the bridge is a heavy clay cutting, 1,500 feet long.

The next station is St. Octave, 561 feet above sea level. The settlement is small and unimportant. Twelve miles from here, by the road, is Grand Metis, first settled by the Scotch in 1818. The arable country is well farmed. At Little Metis, three miles from the station, there is excellent fishing and bathing. At time of writing there are 400 visitors at this place. Here we lose sight of the St. Lawrence, which has kept us company so long, and turn inland. Between this point and 19 miles east, are

SIX LARGE CUTTINGS,

over which snow sheds have been built, cut through solid rock in almost
every instance, representing a total of five thousand eight hundred feet of
excavation. The following table will show the mileage, length and depth
of these sheds ;—

Distances from Riviere du Loup.	Stations.	Length	Depth.
Miles.		Feet.	Feet.
89	4 miles west of St. Octave.	1200	28
93	St. Octave.	3000	35
94	1 mile east of St. Octave.	200	29
95	2 miles " " "	500	38
98	5 " " " "	700	28
100	7 " " " "	200	35

On section 13, through which these cuttings run, there are 246,600 cubic
feet of rock, and 1,509,900 of earth excavation.

There is some high land between St. Octave and the next station, at the
98th mile from Riviere du Loup, which is 708 feet above sea level.

Tartague is the next stopping place, 10 miles from St. Octave. Its
elevation is 565 feet.

To save space, I append a list of stations and bridges and snow sheds
between Tartague and Mill Stream :—

Distance from Riviere du Loup.	Stations.	Elevation above Sea Level.
Miles.		Feet.
113	Sayabec......................	573
120	Cedar Hill.................	540
128	Amqui, opposite Lake Metapedia	537
141	Causaposcal......................	446
156	Assametquaghan..................	265
166	Mill Stream..................	166

Between these points are the following

IRON BRIDGES.

Quarter mile west of Sayabec, over the Sayabec River, one span of 24
feet.

One mile east of Sayabec station, one span of 80 feet, over the St. Pierre
river.

Four miles east of Cedar Hill station, one span of 80 feet over the
Tobagot river.

One half mile east of Amqui station, three spans of 50 feet each, over
Indian Brook, a tributary of the Metapedia..

At Causaposcal station, over the Metapedia river, a "skew" bridge built at an angle of forty-five degrees to the line of railway, three spans of 100 feet each.

Five miles east of Causaposcal, over the same river, three spans of 100 feet built at an angle of forty-five degrees.

Four miles east of Assametquagban, three spans of sixty feet each, over McKinnon's Brook.

Two miles west of Mill Stream station, over the Metapedia, four spans, each of 100 feet, built on the "skew."

SNOW SHEDS.

The only snow sheds between Tartague and Mill Stream are :—

Five miles east of Tartague, 400 feet long and twenty feet deep.

The second is five miles east of Amqui station, 600 feet long and 20 feet deep.

The highest elevation between St Octave and Mill Stream is at Lake Malafat, half way between Tartague and Sayabec, at the 188th mile, of 743 feet above the sea. Causaposcal is the only station between St. Octave and Mill Stream which has a building. Tenders, however, are are being given for the construction of others as soon as possible. The descent from the cars into the cheerless spaces at which you suppose you are going to find a platform and depot is not inviting. Surrounded by rock, mountain and crag, not even a sign of human life to meet you, is not calculated to arouse the spirits even of the most sanguine of mortals. In wet weather the mud is plentiful and adhesive.

In addition to the cuttings already given between St. Octave and Mill Stream there are

NINE TUNNELS

under the line, eight of which were driven through the rock to save masonry for culverts. Two are 12 feet, one is 9 feet, and five are 6 feet in diameter. The largest is 227 feet long, and the excavation 908 cubic yards. The others are from 69 to 190 feet long. Perhaps the one most dfficult of construction is that by which the Tartague stream is diverted. This is 18 x 20 feet, 454 feet long, and the excavation is 4,540 cubic yards. The total excavation represented by these nine tunnels, is 6,745, and to their approaches 14,000 cubic yards. In the diversion of the river alone there were excavations of 7,500 cubic yards of rock, and 20,654 cubic yards of earth.

When the reader has well digested these facts he will be able to form some idea of the enormous difficulties which have had to be surmounted in the construction of this portion of the line.

Leaving Mill Stream station we travel ten miles further and arrive at

THE METAPEDIAC.

The station is about 39 feet above the sea level. It is approached by a bridge o   le pattern, constructed of rolled plates and flat iron struts. It has five spans of 200 feet each, and crosses the Restigouche. Seven miles east of the station is another of seven spans of 600 feet each, crossing Christopher's Brook.

The course of the line from St. Octave, when you leave the St. Lawrence is south by west until you come to Lake Malafat, between Tartague and Sayabec. This lake is about a quarter of a mile long and half a mile wide. You continue twelve miles east by south, when you sight the Metapdia Lake about half way from its centre. It is sixteen miles long. You then strike Salmon Lake, 15 miles distant. The latter is in reality a swelling of the river which flows through it.

After crossing the Restigouche you are in the Province of New Brunswick. The Valley of the Metapediac will probably be within five years from now the best known country in the Dominion. It is seventy miles long ; extending from Restigouche to the lake. The line of railway closely follows the course of the river. The nature of the surrounding country is not favorable to the location of a line of railway ; but civilization is indebted to science for an acquaintance with this picturesque country. The cost of construction of some portions of the line along the valley, which required heavy masonry, and which necessitated the hauling of large blocks of stone, was at the rate of $70,000 per mile. At Mill Stream and at Mann's Hill you will find embankments built on slopes from 150 to 200 feet, and which contain from 70,000 to 80,000 cubic yards of excavation. Solid rock, cuttings from 20 to 46 feet in depth are frequently encountered.

The valley for about half its distance is not more than half a mile wide, and is traversed by the Metapedia road, a military highway built by the Government in 1862. It is on the east side of the river, and extends from Cross Point to St. Flavie. The hills along the valley, which range commences above the source of the river at Grand Lake, are mostly conical in shape, of an altitude of from 500 to 900 feet. The windings of the river, as you catch the sun's reflection from time to time upon it, resemble some huge but graceful silvery snake whose lustrous scales give back a million scintilations. The scenery through the valley is more grandly picturesque at sunrise and sunset, when you have Nature robed in all her golden splendor. The river rises in Lake Metapedia, 20 miles from the St. Lawrence, and is surrounded by a well wooded country. Along the Lake Metapediac, there are numerous small islands, irregular in shape but beautiful in appearance. The Indian meaning of the Metapediac river, is "musical waters." Its principal tributaries are the Amqui, Causaposcal, Assametquaghan and Mill Stream. The Causaposcal forms a junction with the main river and is also known as the Forks. The land in rear of the mountains is said to be good along the area of the valley ; but it would not pay as a settlement. There are over 200 rapids along the Metapediac, some of which are so swift that none but an experienced canoe oarsman dare venture over them. To write up the valley of the Metapediac as it should be written would need a small volume. Justice cannot be done to the subject in a single letter. The village, though small, is excellently adapted for farming purposes but within a limited area. The population is about 400.

"CAMPING OUT"

The following sketch will give the reader a good idea of the attraction held out to tourists and anglers :—

After the summit level is passed the train descends at the rate of 40 miles an hour down the valley of the Metapediac and along the banks of that beautiful river. As the train flies along down the valley, we fear we are likely to run in the river alongside of us. But the road-bed is good, and the steel rails make the bed of the road like a billiard table. So we are landed at the Metapediac station, opposite our friend Daniel Fraser's hospitble door, before we realize that we are out of the Province of Quebec. The Valley of the Metapediac contains some of the finest scenery in the Dominion, and as the air is cool and good fishing is to be had here, I would advise tourists or invalids to take a trip to the delightful place by cars, and he or they could not be disappointed.

We met a party of gentlemen from St. John and New York at Dalhousie *en route* for fishing quarters on the grand Cascapedia, the other side of the Bay of Chaleur. They had a tug steamer hired to take them over (35 miles), and offered us a passage with them, which would take us very near the mouth of the little Cascapedia ; but when the time of sailing arrived and no appearance of the steamer, we took the opportunity of a fair wind and tide and the offer of a good boat, and arrived at our destination in 3½ hours, after a glorious sail down the Bay.

On Monday morning we had our two birch canoes and four men ready to ascend the river 20 miles. Loading a canoe with our baggage and provisions for 14 days, we started on our way up the river in the direction of the Shick Shock mountain, and arrived at our camp at 6 p.m., after a hard day's pulling. Some of the rapids look very ugly to a person not accustomed to this mode of travel. Having built a large shanty 30 by 20 feet the first time we came here, we soon found ourselves at home in this wild, mountainous place, distant 18 miles from the nearest house.

The air was bracing, and the river water as clear as crystal, and as cold as ice. Next morning, after a good bath in the river, which made our teeth chatter, we started to fish, and went up ten miles to the foot of the river, where the principal spawning beds of the salmon are. We had very fine sea trout fishing for the rest of the week, the fish weighing five pounds each, and gave excellent sport in landing them.

On Saturday we went down to New Richmond, and on the way netted forty-three trout and three salmon, of about twenty-pounds each.

On the following Tuesday I went up the river about eight miles, and got two salmon and forty trout, averaging as above in weight, and altogether, we got in seven days fourteen salmon, and 800 pounds of very fine trout, of which we pickled two barrels, after giving to our friends as much more fresh.

On our way up the river we saw a very large eagle rising from off an island in front of us, and on landing we found the remains of a dead rabbit, on which the monarch of birds was making his dinner. We also saw the fresh track of moose and deer on the island opposite our camp. One of our Indians, (Black John) one evening went from the camp a short distance in search of birch bark to make a canoe, when he came to a large tree, newly-stripped of its outer bark by a bear, to get at the inner bark, of which he is very fond.

On our way down the river our men told us of

A BEAVER DAM,

four hundred yards from the bank of the river. So, being anxious to see it, we took the things out of one of the canoes, and in a trice the four men had it on their shoulders, and off we started for the beaver dam. We very soon arrived at a large sheet of water, about half a mile in length, formed by the beavers felling large trees, some 14 to 18 inches in diameter across the lower end, and then smaller timber laid at an angle of 45 degrees into the ground, with their upper ends restin n the cross beams. They then fill up between with clay and small sticks, till the dam is as tight as a drum. Near the upper end they have two houses, one about 12 feet in diameter and the other about eight feet (which, I presume, is the ladies' house or nursery). The entrance to these houses is from below water and the shape conical or very like a cock of hay. The bottom of the dam is covered with a beautiful green carpet of moss, and as the water is very clear, you can see ridges along the bottom and holes in them where the beaver makes himself at home when he is afraid of man or gets tired of his two story castle.

On examining the chips which these creatures cut from the trees they had felled, I found some of them 4 to 5 inches long, and cut as if with a woodman's axe.

Having engaged our schooner to come back for us on Saturday, to the mouth of the river, we arrived dripping with wet, but in excellent health and with good appetites. We found our skipper just arrived and ready for us. At 5 o'clock next morning we hoisted sail, and with a fair wind and delicious trip arrived at Dalhousie the same afternoon.

No. VI.

CAMPBELLTON AND DALHOUSIE.

After riding through thirteen miles of charming country Campbellton is reached. It is located almost at the foot of the Sugar Loaf Mountain, 996 feet high, by actual measurement. Between Metapedia station and Campbellton there is a cutting 400 feet long and 25 wide. It is difficult to say which is the more beautiful river, the Restigouche or the Metapedia, which we have left behind us. The line of railway follows the course of the river. The Restigouche river is in the county of Madawaska. It is 220 miles long, and for half that distance it forms the dividing line between the Provinces of Quebec and New Brunswick. Five rivers empty into it, of which the chief are the Metapediac, the Cascapediac and the Gautawam-kedgwick. The Restigouche empties into the Bay Chaleur, and flows through an extensive timber tract. The river gives employment to a number of fishermen, who derive their maintenance from the abundance of salmon, trout, etc., which is to be be found in its waters. Large vessels can navigate it to within thirty miles from its mouth. The Bonaventure mountains extend along its narrow shore, and give the eye every variety of landscape it can desire, filling the mind with wonder and admiration for their magnificent and wild beauty.

The town of Campbellton is small, and its population does not exceed 600 persons. The Intercolonial will, however, be the means of adding materially to its prosperity. Already several new stores are in course of erection, and the general business air of the townsfolk strikes you favorably. Many of them are Scotch settlers, thrifty and pushing.

There are several Government buildings in the vicinity of the station. The station is of brick, and is occupied by the railroad cashier, Molson's Bank agency, offices of the Assistant Superintendent, Chief Engineer's office, the living apartments of the Station Master, beside the usual ticket office, waiting rooms, &c. A refreshment room has been added to the station. North of the station house is the freight house. On the opposite side of the track is the blacksmith's shop, the coal shed, the oil house, engine house and car shop.

Campbellton is full of historical and local interest. It has two churches —the Presbyterian and Roman Catholic. The former is the first Protestant church east of Cacouna, 183 miles west. I had the pleasure of meeting two gentlemen who are the sons of the first white woman of British parents born in this section. The gentlemen to whom I refer are A. Ferguson and Robert Ferguson, Esquires, Conservatives of the old school. Their names are so well known along the whole line that I am sure they will be recognized at once by a large number of persons. Both are bachelors and keep open house with that generous hospitality typical of the English squire. Although well advanced in years, they are stout, strong and vigorous.

The Messrs. Ferguson own a large fishery in front of their property.

The farms here are in excellent order. For the sake of comparison I obtained the

AVERAGE YIELD PER ACRE

of the various crops, and append a list, so that you may see how it compares with those at Trois Pistoles, where, you will remember, I obtained a similar statement.

Barley gives an average of 10 bushels per acre; rye 10 bushels; wheat 8 bushels; potatoes 24½ barrels to one barrel of seed. The figures with regard to oats and buckwheat I was unable to procure, but I am told they are very satisfactory

There are two salmon canning establishments here, but they are not in operation at present. The first is owned by Mr Hoegg, of Portland, Maine, just at the brck of the station; the second by Mr. Haddow, of Dalhousie, four miles east of Campbellton. To accomodate this trade the Government has constructed six refrigerator cars, which I saw at the station. They are lined with zinc, and filled in with bark, and appear to be excellent for the purpose.

At Cross Point, on the opposite shore, there is

AN INDIAN MISSION

under the spiritual care of the Roman Catholic Church. The settlement contains about 400 Mic-Macs, the oldest of whom is an old guide named Sam Suke, now about seventy-eight years of age. They are a quiet faithful people. The Government recently gave them 10,000 acres of wooded land; but beside this they have about 200 acres well under cultivation. Their Church is a neat edifice, and the settlement from the New Brunswick side looks like a thriving, picturesque town, very level but well sheltered.

Perhaps the most attractive feature of Campbellton is its

HISTORIC INTEREST.

In its immediate vicinity there are the remains of five French vessels of war which were sunk during the year 1760. The first two are at Old Church Point, at the head of the tide, three miles from Campbellton on the Quebec side; there are also two at Bourdon opposite the Ferguson property, and one at Cross Point. Others are reported to be sunk in the channel some ten miles from the mouth of the river. They were sunk and burned by the French themselves in order to impede the progress of the British fleet under Commodore Byron from ascending the river. The remains of a portion of the wreck off Old Church Point can be seen at low water, but time has so firmly fastened its timbers in the river's bed that it is impossible to investigate its interior. Mr. Adam Ferguson has in his possession two iron 18-pounders from these vessels. One is of twisted iron, apparently hammered, the other is cast. They have the *fleur de lys* of France stamped upon them, and are covered with, and partly eaten away by rust. The same gentleman has a swivel gun captured from an American privateer during the war of 1812, which bears the broad arrow mark. As the country became cleared, the settlers found cannon balls imbedded in the trees and earth. They account for the fact by supposing that the guns were loaded before the vessels were fired, as no fighting took place at this point.

Mr. Lefebvre, of Carleton, 30 miles from here, has or had

A CURIOUS INDIAN RELIC

which merits a description. While the Metapediac military road (already referred to in my last letter) was being built on the Quebec side, six miles from Campbellton, the workmen, in excavating the bank, came across the remains of what was supposed to be an Indian. The head reposed on a clear cut triangle of stone. On the region of the heart of the skeleton was a small marble ornament, suspended by a metal chain, either of copper or brass, very much corroded. The ornament is cut from a piece of greenish-blue marble, perfectly smooth. It is six inches long, and in shape similar to a whip-saw file. By the side of the remains there was also found a metal chisel or axe, something like a ship carpenter's hawsying iron. These are the only pieces of metal ever found in this part of the country. Their discovery has given rise to much speculation, and some associate the articles with Freemasonry. It may be that this is correct, for I heard from an army officer in Kansas that his life was once saved by a Sioux Indian who appeared familiar with several Masonic signs. The fact however, is one in which antiquaries will find ample scope for conjecture.

It was with regret that I was compelled to leave this charming country, replete with delightful scenery and romantic incident, and proverbially hospitable. Before closing my description, it may surprise your musical readers to learn that young ladies who have never been fifty miles away from it in their lives are familiar with Thalberg's pianoforte studies. Fancy hearing operatic *morceaux* in this country of rocks, hills and primitive simplicity! Campbellton will always be gratefully remembered by your correspondent.

DALHOUSIE.

Dalhousie station is nine miles east of here. It is seventy feet above sea level. One mile east of Campbellton station you cross another iron bridge of three spans of sixty feet each over Mile Creek. The nature of the country remains the same, so I will not recapitulate the superb scenery to which no person can do justice. The track here is as good as ever; but the ballasting is not yet complete. The rails are as smooth and as even as a billiard-table ; the work being substantial and thorough.

The town of Dalhousie is on the beautiful Baie des Chaleur, seven miles distant, over a rocky, uncomfortable road, full of ruts and mire. I remained there with the firm conviction that I had placed the mosquitoes under deep obligation for considerable nutriment. If they hadn't obtained the traditional ounce of flesh, they certainly had no reason to complain of not getting enough blood. Mosquitoes have that keen sense of perception which enables them to scent a stranger half an hour before the cars arrive, and you find them waiting to receive you. They need no introduction because they introduce themselves. If any one was desirous of ascertaining the nature of this country, he need only look at my swollen features to get a tolerably fair idea of its rugged nature. My lineaments are all hills and valleys. Seriously speaking, the mosquitoes are an unmitigated nuisance.

The railway runs back from Eel River to Shore's Cove for six miles, nearly in a straight line. The people feel very sore at its omitting to touch the town. But this would have necessitated an additional distance of three miles through costly cuttings, which would have had to be made. The direction which the people desired was as follows :—Crossing Eel River

Bay, running around the shore to Dalhousie lighthouse, passing by the **Hamilton** monument (to which reference will be made directly), through the town and along the bank of the Restigouche to the present station. I understand that offers have been made by contractors to build a branch line for $50,000, but it is questionable whether a good road could be built for this amount. At any rate, if the Dalhousians ever wish to avail themselves of the natural advantages the place possesses, and which would be increased fifty per cent., this line will have to be built, and until it is the Intercolonial will be of but little use to them.

I have said the town is situated at a point on the Baie des Chaleur. It is bounded west and north by the Restigouche, on the east by the Bay, and on the south by the back country. It is naturally and admirably fitted for a deep water terminus.

Its population is about 1,200. The town has an area of five miles. The principal industry is lumber, which yields an average of 15,000,000 per year, and 3,000 tons of square timber, principally spruce and birch. The principal lumber merchant is George Moffatt, Esq , M.P., Conservative. He owns a large saw mill here.

POINTS OF INTEREST.

Hamilton monument. This was erected by the inhabitants in memory of the first merchant of Dalhousie. Indeed, the town was originally named after him. It is said to be the largest monument erected to a private individual in the Dominion. It stands on Dalhousie Hill, from which may be seen the harbor, and the different churches, viz., the Episcopal, the Roman Catholic, and the Presbyterian. Numerous drives and walks can be seen from this elevation. Fossil remains were discovered about two years ago south-east of the town. Along the coast and within a quarter cf a mile of Dalhousie, there is abundance of herring, cod, eel and salmon.

HAMILTON'S MONUMENT

is of free stone. It was cut in Glasgow, Scotland, and erected in 1851. It stands 20 feet high, and bears the following inscription :—

In memory of
CAPTAIN JOHN HAMILTON,
a native of King's Cross, Arran, Scotland.
He was the first merchant who
settled at Dalhousie, and along with
many benevolent actions, built St. John's
Presbyterian Church, for which
his friends and countrymen here thus record
their gratitude.
He passed the last 10 years of his
life in his native land
and died at Irvine, 24th August, 1868.
Aged 80 years.

You will be able to form a pretty good idea of the economical tendencies of the people of Dalhousie when I tell you that the Government District Saving's Bank received deposits in the county last year amounting to $120,000, exclusive of money held in Government bonds. The money order office alone did the largest business of any office within New Brunswick, not excepting St. John, up to last year. This may be accounted for by the absence of any local banking branch in the town. The population in the county is about 5,000.

It is estimated that in 1874 there was probably 400,000 pounds of salmon put up within the county of Restigouche, and about the same quantity of lobsters. (By the way, the shells of the latter are extensively used by some farmers as manure. They say it makes an excellent article.) There are four persons engaged in the lobster and salmon business, viz., Mr. George Haddow, Mr. Hoegg, Mr. Windsor, at Campbellton and New Mills, and Mr. Bain, also at the latter place. New Mills is sixteen miles east of Dalhousie and will be referred to at the proper time. The advantage of Dalhousie, situated as it is, will at once be apparent to the reader if he will only look at its situation on the map. I only regret that my time will not permit of a further description of this lovely point, which from nearly every side is exceedingly beautiful.

NO. VII.

FROM DALHOUSIE TO BATHURST.

Before the traveller reaches Bathurst from Dalhousie he passes five stations, the vicinity of each being noted, more or less, for its salmon fishing. These stations are—

Charlo, ten miles east of Dalhousie, forty-five feet above sea level. Half way between it and Dalhousie there is an iron bridge, with a single span of 100 feet, over Eel River. One mile east of Charlo Station there is another bridge over the Charlo River, which empties into the Baie des Chaleurs, of three spans of fifty feet each; and within a few hundred feet there is a third bridge of two spans of fifty feet each.

New Mills is the second station, and is thirty feet above the sea level. Half a mile east of it is a bridge of two spans, each sixty feet, over the Benjamin River, which also empties into the Baie des Chaleurs.

Six miles east of New Mills we come to another bridge of a single span of eighty feet, over Nash's Creek; and a mile distant from the same, crossing Louison's Brook, is one of sixty feet.

Jacquet River is the next station, nine miles from Charlo. It has an elevation of forty-one feet. At the 227th mile from Riviere du Loup, the level rises to 227 feet above the sea. I should have mentioned that at one mile west of the station there is a bridge of 300 feet in length—three spans, of 100 feet each. Four miles east of the station is another, crossing the Belledune River, of a single span of eighty feet.

Belledune Station, nine miles from the former, is built at an elevation of eighty feet. Two miles east of it is a snow-shed 300 feet long and fifteen feet deep. Near it, is another snow-shed 600 feet long and eighteen feet deep.

The next station is Petit Roche, eight miles from the former, at a sea level of eighty-nine feet. Two miles west of it a bridge, with a single span of eighty feet, crosses Elm Tree River. Three miles east of the station, over the Nigados River, is a bridge with a single span of eighty feet. At the 238th mile from Riviere du Loup are two cuttings, or snow-sheds: the first 1,000 feet long and twenty-five feet deep; the second 378 feet long and twenty feet deep. This latter completes the number of snow-sheds, which gives a total of fifteen, representing 10,978 yards of excavation, mostly through solid rock, between St. Fabian and this point. The average depth of these cuttings is twenty-six and a half feet. These facts may appear rather dry reading, but they speak of gigantic difficulties overcome, of long days of mental study and of many months of toil and labor. Dry as they may appear to some, they tell their tale of successful engineering skill of which modern science may well be proud.

Three miles west of Bathurst Station a bridge of five spans, of 100 feet each and seventy feet high, crosses the Tete-a-gouche. It is a splendid structure of the lattice girder pattern. The piers and abutments contain 2,400 cubic yards of solid masonry. The rails on the bridge are sixty-five feet from the river bed.

It would take too long to go thoroughly into the question of the construction of these bridges, which would only interest professional men. However, the general reader has a sufficient description of them to form a faint notion of the quality and quantity of the work along the line. The above stations have the same neat appearance which those west of Campbellton possess, though much smaller.

Twelve miles from Petit Roche and 252 from Riviere du Loup is

BATHURST.

The station is at an elevation of thirty-five feet above the sea. The building is built of brick, sixty-six feet long and thirty feet wide. It is built upon a stone foundation. The town is one and a quarter mile from the station. It was originally settled in the year 1780 by three French settlers named Hache, Doucette, and D'Aigle. The early history of New Brunswick is closely identified with the place. The reader, if she or he be so minded, would do well to study its history, which abounds with historical romance exceedingly interesting. My only desire, however, is rather to deal with the present age, and to tell what it has achieved in this era of progress and competition.

Bathurst, Gloucester County, is situated to the east of the station, and is built on the shores of the harbor of Bathurst Bay, into which the rivers Nipisiguit, Tete-a-gouche, Middle River and Little River flow. These streams are not tributaries, but independent rivers. The harbor is a beautiful sheet of water, as smooth as glass, and affords capital boating. The harbor is two and a half miles in diameter, and is entered from Nipisiguit Bay, which is nearly landlocked, and forms a portion of the Baie des Chaleurs. The channel, fourteen feet deep, runs between Carron and Alston points, three miles from the town. That portion of the harbor above the bridge, which connects the town with the village of St. Peter's (by which name it is said Bathurst was originally called), is named the Basin. This bridge is half a mile long. It may be stated that in order to make the railway more convenient, a project has been mooted for the construction of another bridge from the foot of the principal street (Water street) directly across to the railway station through the diameter of the circle. This is alleged to be necessary to meet the requirements of the business men. Ten thousand dollars, it is thought, would be sufficient for the purpose, and application to the Dominion Government is contemplated to meet this want. This improvement would shorten the distance to the town by half a mile.

The town covers an area of a mile square. It is built on a peninsula, and contains a population of 1,200 persons. It is governed by the municipality of the parish, and sends two representatives to that body. Its local member in the Provincial Government is F. K. Burns, Esq , who is opposed to the general policy of the Administration. The town is judiciously planned, and the streets all run at right angles, and are well built. There are about a dozen streets in all.

At the point at which the Nipisiguit enters the harbor, a bridge 700 feet long is built. The river has a sufficient depth of water to permit of navigation two miles above its mouth. Near it the water dashes boldly along the shore—on the town side. The locality is favorable for milling purposes, and would be well supplied with lumber from the banks of the river, which, throughout its course of 100 miles, is well timbered with pine and spruce of good quality. From the vicinity of the other rivers large supplies could be had.

POINTS OF INTEREST.

Excellent fishing can be had at Rough Waters, the Railway Bridge, Round Rocks, Papineau Falls, Middle Landing ; at the Little and Big Chain of Rocks, and at Grand Falls. The latter place is twenty miles from Bathurst, above which no salmon can ascend. Tourists are pouring in from all parts of the country. I met a company of gentlemen from Halifax, St. John and Montreal, all eager for sport, faithful disciples of the lamented Izaak. At all these places I have mentioned there are fishing pools, and the scenery is in keeping with the beauty of the town, which for quiet, rural and simple loveliness is unsurpassed anywhere in the Province. The view of Grand Falls is very charming. It is approached through a narrow gorge, one and a half miles long, between tall, towering cliffs, which cast their shadows across the stream. In some places the sun never shines upon it. The water is as smooth as glass, and the retreat is one where a love-sick maiden could pine away and die with perfect success.

If you want a good drive, you have your choice of the Bay Shore, Caᵀ ron, or Alston Points, where, if you feel inclined, you may bathe, or fish for cod. A drive around the Basin also would well repay you, crossing the Little and Middle Rivers to enable you to get a splendid view from Rocky Bridge. If you are fond of agricultural scenery you can find it along the Tete-a-gouche River, passing the splendid farm and the former summer residence of the late Francis Ferguson, Esq. Here you can estimate at its proper value the agricultural wealth of the country—notably the well cultivated and richly stocked farm of Hon. John Ferguson. This farm is said to be the finest in the Province, and contains nearly 400 acres under the most approved system of cultivation. The Court House and jail, now famous in connection with the trial of the Caraquet rioters, can be seen from the hill. The former is a substantial building and a credit to the town. If these are not enough attractions, there are others, *ad libitum.*

COMMERCIAL.

The preserving and canning of salmon forms the most important commercial item at present. Large quantities were caught along the bay shore, half of which was previous to this year canned for exportation, principally to England. As much as 400,000 pounds were sent out of the country.

There being no banking facilities, merchants are obliged to transact their businesss at a considerable disadvantage, having to handle their paper, both payable and receivable, principally through two distant banks which, they say, offers them little or no accommodation. Thus, in buying or selling exchange or drafts or *vice versa*, the merchant has to pay 8 per cent., and often a commission of ¼ per cent. added. The smaller merchants transact their financial affairs through the Money Order Department. It is estimated that goods to the amount of $300,000 are sold annually in the town.

The system of long credits and barter heretofore, through necessity, observed, is now rapidly giving way to a ready money basis, from which all parties are beginning to derive a marked benefit. Business here is healthy, imports being light and the demand steady. This demand is stimulated by the Intercolonial. The prospects of more than an average crop are encouraging. The town is also deriving its share of income from the large number of tourists who pour in from all quarters.

In the trade of canned fish, Bathurst is probably one of the most important stations along the North Shore. The largest firms in this branch of business are Messrs. Ferguson, Rankine & Co., Windsor, and others. The quantity of lobsters put up this year, it is thought, will exceed that of salmon, owing to the fact that most of the latter have been exported fresh by rail. Among the larger exporters are Messrs. Baldwin & Molloy, R. Armstrong and Enoch Pifer. These parties use

FISH FREEZERS,

by which they are enabled to hold their fish until the market offers favorable inducements for their sale.

The one in use, by Messrs. Baldwin & Molloy, is extremely ingenious and simple in its construction. It merely consists of two refrigerator vaults, 20 feet long, 12 feet wide, and 8½ feet high. Each vault is a separate chamber. The first contains 20 pipes, 14 inches in diameter; the second, the same number of pipes of an equal diameter, and three cylinders of a diameter of 12 inches. These pipes are fed with ice and salt from the top, and around the side ot these chambers is a trough, in which it is placed. The walls are, on one side, 15 inches thick; well lined with sawdust, and on the other 2 feet in thickness. It will hold 3,000 salmon, and by some secret process, the fish retains its natural color and brightness. At the time of my visit, there were about fifteen hundred salmon in store, weighing from 8 to 30 pounds. The temperature depends upon the regularity and quantity of the supply of ice and salt. The interior was arranged with trays, upon which the fish were placed, and the thermometer registered 18° above zero, although it is often as low as 16° Coming out of the open air, with the thermometer at 87° in the shade, into this intensely cold atmosphere, the shock to the system was exceedingly telling. The cold strikes into your bones, and it was several hours before the chill left me. It was so cold that an inch of snow encrusted the exterior of the pipes. This invention is patented, and could be made to apply to household purposes. I saw some fine mackerel here, weighing from two to three pounds, selling for two cents each.

GENERAL REMARKS.

The predominating creed here is the Roman Catholic, although there are in addition to the Roman Catholic Church, the churches of the Episcopalian, Presbyterian and Methodist denominations. The Conservative element is gaining strength. The Free School question is the most important subject of local and provincial politics. A concession, I believe, was obtained from the Provincial Board of Education last year by the local representative, whereby the Catholic ratepayers should receive some benefit from the object for which the people are taxed. With one exception, the hotel accommodation is only middling, and that exception is the Wilbur House, a good, comfortable hotel, which is scarcely large enough for the number of visitors who go there.

NO. VII.

FROM BATHURST TO MIRAMICHI.

Before writing of the Miramichi district, which includes the towns of Chatham and Newcastle, mention must be made of the work along the road.

There are three stations between these points, a distance of forty-four miles.

The first is

Red Pine, three hundred and thirty-one feet above sea level, but before this is reached you cross a bridge three miles east of Bathurst Station, over Little River. It is a single span of sixty feet. Two miles further is another, crossing the Nipisiguit River, of six spans, of one hundred feet each and thirty-eight feet above the river. This is a lattice girder. The masonry is of granite, and the piers and abutments are founded in solid rock. The cost of the bridge alone was $60,000. Five miles west of Red Pine, and crossing the brook of that name is a plate-girder bridge, with three spans of forty feet each. The granite masonry appears to be built to last till doomsday, and gives evidence of thoroughly finished work. The structure is handsome and imposing, and affords a fine photographic study. On this section (16) there is a total of 2,318 yards of first-class masonry, 955 yards of second-class, and 350,000 yards of earth cuttings.

The next station is Bartibogue, 514 feet elevation above the sea. This is the highest point between Bathurst and Newcastle. Four miles east of the station and crossing the Bartibogue river, which empties into the Bay Chaleur, is a lattice girder bridge, with a single span of eighty feet, approached from the east by an embankment containing 60,000 cubic yards of earth. One mile west of the next station, you pass through a rock cutting one and a quarter mile long, containing 125,000 cubic yards, and near by there is an embankment containing 60,000 cubic yards.

The third station is Beaver Brook, at an elevation, above sea level, of three hundred and twenty-four feet.

The line along this portion of the road is nearly straight, passing through a dull, uninteresting country, which, in contrast to the beautiful character of the landscapes through which you have travelled, heightens your appreciation of the splendid views left behind.

Ten miles from Beaver Brook you arrive at Miramichi Station. It is one hundred and thirty-one feet above sea level. The water is supplied from a brook, nearly two miles distant, by a reservoir six hundred by two hundred and fifty feet. Its construction cost $10,000.

THE MIRAMICHI DISTRICT.

The celebrated lumber reigon traversed by the Miramichi river, which drains 6,000 square miles of territory, is so well known by repute that it does not need more than a passing mention of its principal features. The river is divided into the North-west and South-west branches. The head-waters of the latter are in Northumberland county, near the Nipisiguit. The former takes its rise in the lakes of Victoria and Carleton counties. The greatest depth of the Miramichi, where its branches unite, is above Newcastle. From here it gradually widens into the Bay of Miramichi, and eventually flows into the great Gulf of the St. Lawrence. The area of Miramichi proper is about 2,000 miles. It is with regret that time will not permit of dwelling upon the historical associations of this district, the first grant of which dates back 1690, to one Denis de Frousac. Cartier's name is closely associated with this tract of country, the timber from which has found its way into all parts of the civilized world.

THE GREAT FIRE OF OCTOBER, 1825,

will always form a part of the most notable portion of the history of New Brunswick. That vast forest of flame, one hundred miles in length, destroyed 8,000 square miles of country a million dollars worth of property, the lives of 200 persons, nine hundred head of cattle and five hundred buildings. Newcastle was burnt to the ground. Mr. W. K. Reynolds, Jr. of St. John, N. B., has written a graphic history of this fearful disaster—probably the greatest fire in area the world has ever known. In it he gives many interesting particulars, and from it we take the above facts—the number of persons excepted.

NEWCASTLE

is one-fourth of a mile from, and southeast of the station. It is about a mile square, and has a population of nearly 2,000 persons. It stands on the westerly bank of the Miramichi.

The principal industry is lumber. In the the town there are two saw mills, with a cutting capacity of from 40,000 to 60,000 feet per day, principally of spruce timber.

The largest mill owners are Messrs. D. & J. Ritchie & Co. and W. Park, Esq. Lumbermen over at the mills earn from $1.50 to $2.00 per day.

The following

CUSTOM HOUSE RETURNS OF LUMBER EXPORTS FOR JUNE, 1876,

will enable the reader to arrive at an approximate idea of this branch of industry.

The exports to the European markets, chiefly England, were :—

	Feet.
Batiens	89,052
Deals	8,010,925
Deal ends	279,011
Scantling	479,982
Boards	34,531
Palings	420,750
	Tons.
Birch	30

The coastwise exports, mostly to the United States were :—

	Feet.
Deals	273,341
Deal ends	4,000
Scantlings	1,700
Boards	109,717
Palings	23,825
Laths	238,500
Shingles	47,750

It should be mentioned that this does not represent all the lumber properly within the port of Newcastle, for in addition to those mills referred to there are three others that cut lumber for Chatham merchants, the products being entered at that port. These would give an additional amount of about 11,000,000 feet per annum.

Owing to the keen competition with the Pacific trade, the canned salmon industry is almost at a stand still, although fresh salmon has been largely supplied during the present year. From June 1st to 14th there were shipped to the United States 309 boxes, containing 5,444 fish, weighing, say, on an average, ten pounds. The largest shippers are Messrs. H. P. & T. Crocker, Mr. E. C. Tozer, and Messrs. Donald Morrison & Co. Large quantities of bass are shipped from the northwest stream, about seven miles west of the Branch. These fish are at times so plentiful that as much as $70 worth have been caught in one night. This occurred a short time ago. Shipments of trout, smelts and eels are also made on a smaller scale.

There is a good-sized wharf in the town, the water being sixteen feet deep at low tide, where two river steamers, owned by Messrs. R. R. Call and John C. Miller, arrive and depart. The latter gentleman owns a hemlock bark-extract factory at Derby, nine miles from Newcastle. One of these vessels, the Era, makes four trips daily between Newcastle and Chatham. There are also two ferries and four steam tugs in operation, which are kept pretty busy during the summer.

The town is lit with gas, apparently of good quality. The works are run at the private cost of Alex. Stewart, who is the proprietor of the best hotel in the place, the Waverley House, which is becoming well known for the excellent comfort which its owner provides for his guests. Newcastle is represented in the County Council, consisting of a warden and twenty-one councillors. The county was incorporated but recently, and met for the first time in January last. The people are Conservatives, and a paper in this interest, the *Union Advocate*, is circulated largely through the county. There are five churches—the Presbyterian, Episcopal, Roman Catholic, Methodist, and Baptist. The first of these predominates.

POINTS OF INTEREST.

There are many picturesque points in the vicinity of Newcastle. One of these is Mill Cove, one mile below Newcastle. On each side is sloping, high land, and a stream of the same name runs through the valley and supplies power to the grist mill owned by the Hon. R. Hutchison. The locality is well wooded with birch and maple groves, whose dazzling tints of autumn foliage are said to be unsurpassed for their richness of color. Beaubair's Island, owned by the Hon. Peter Mitchell, is also another interesting place. It is just below the junction of the branches of the Miramichi River. It is a favorite resort for tourists and pleasure-seekers. Here may be seen the grave of the first British settler, William Davidson, of the Miramichi District, who emigrated thither in 1764, and obtained a large grant of land on the Southwest Branch. He constructed the first schooner built on the Miramichi River in 1773. On his tombstone is the following :

Sacred to the Membry
of
WM. DAVIDSON, ESQ.,
Representative for the County of Northumberland, Province of New Brunswick ; Judge of the Court of Common Pleas ; Contractor for the Masts for His Majesty's Navy. He died on the 17th of June, 1790, aged 50. He was one of the first settlers of the river, and greatly instrumental in promoting the settlement. He left a widow and five children to deplore their loss.
" Memento Mori."

Many of the oldest families in St. John are descendants of the above.

Had I the time I might tell you of many other interesting features in connection with the island.

Good fly-fishing for salmon, trout and gilse may be had at Big Hole, on the Northwest River, fifteen miles distant. The waggon road is fair, and the steamers will carry you within five miles of it.

The people of Newcastle are industrious, thrifty and energetic, as may be seen by the many tasteful residences and handsome churches, which are all on sites favorable for observation. They are hospitable and courteous to strangers, and whether it be amusement or business which receives their attention, they attend to it thoroughly, as the following instance will show :—

HOW THE MIRAMICHI FOLKS AMUSE THEMSELVES.

A picnic was given recently by a local temperance society. The day was hot and dusty. After arriving at their destination, the party waited for somebody to start the amusements. Things were getting "slow," and each waited for the other to enliven the festivities. Among those present were several visitors from other parts of the country. What was to be **done**? The reputation of Newcastle for fun and humor was at stake, and that was a serious consideration. The very thought of such a dreadful calamity threw a funeral tone, as it were, over the company. Whether **the heat** or the ginger "pop" had enervated the party, no one could tell. **In** a fit of desperation, one of the picnickers offered to wager five cents that he could out-roll his friend a distance of fifty yards. The **bet** was taken, **and** the contestants extended themselves at full length upon the grass. Distance was measured, and the signal given. **Now,** these two gentlemen were remarkable opposites in their build and appearance. **One was broad** shouldered, but very thin, tapering down to a point, herring-fashion. The other was large, bulky and robust, like a tommy-cod. The race commenced with the thermometer almost 90 ° in the shade. What the **thin man lacked in fatness, he made** up in speed; but his fat rival gained an impetus from his very roundness of body. All *he* had to do was to give himself a jerk every once in a while, and roll himself by the mere force of his own momentum. It was a curious and instructive sight to see the deliberate air of gravity which settled upon the features of the two parties. Not a smile to relieve the business-like air which fastened upon their perspiring countenances. The thin man looked furiously determined, and gained a foot ahead at the start. The fat man, with compressed lips and serious mien, gave himself an **extra** jerk, and made up the lost distance. The thin man got excited, and scratched his nose badly. The fat man kept on and won the race. It was then a question for the judges to decide whether the extra size of **the fat man's body should not be allowed to the thin man on the start.** But it was ably argued that this would not have been just, because the fat man, although larger than his rival, **required more strength to roll successfully.** However, the defeat of the thin man was repeated in two subsequent races, and the facts are merely mentioned to show that when Newcastle men set about doing a thing, they do it thoroughly, even at a picnic.

No. IX.

FROM MIRAMICHI STATION TO CHATHAM JUNCTION.

From Miramichi Station to Chatham Junction is six miles, and three miles east of the former an iron bridge of the Phœnixville pattern, 1,200 feet long, of six spans, crosses the north-west branch of the Miramichi River. This is the only structure between the two points; but it affords a splendid view and is an excellent specimen of massive masonry.

There is much to be said about Chatham itself, that I cannot give but a small space to the mention of the scenery along the line. Suffice it to say it is rugged and bare of noteworthy remark, although it is somewhat peculiar from its very weediness—so to speak.

The town of

CHATHAM

is on the south side of Miramichi River, in the County of Northumberland. It is the largest town on the North Shore, and has a population of 4,000. The position of the town is direct north of the station, about half a mile distant. Its approach by the river, coming from Newcastle, impresses you favorably by its business-like appearance and commodious wharves. There is a general air of sprightliness about it very pleasing to the stranger. The largest wharf is 900 feet long, with a depth of water at low tide, at one place of twenty feet, and at another of twenty-seven feet.

The town is built on a gentle slope. The streets are at right angles and are broad, and well made. The principal street (Water street,) forms part of the high road. It extends a distance of about a mile in the town, and is about sixty feet wide. It is well lighted with gas,—far superior in brilliancy to our Montreal gas—has good sidewalks, and the shops are spacious and imposing. The second principal street is Wellington street, running parallel with the former and is sixty-six feet wide. The lower end of the town is encircled by one small hill in its rear, from which a capital view may be had of the town and surrounding country.

RELIGIOUS, EDUCATIONAL AND SOCIAL.

Chatham is well supplied with churches. It has two Presbyterian, one Episcopalian, one Methodist, and the Roman Catholic cathedral of the diocese, in connection with which is a college and convent, both largely patronized. The schools are divided into three districts; three schools in each, besides a high school and a grammar school. The principal buildings are the Mechanics' Institute and the Masonic Hall, both extremely creditable structures. In addition to the usual temperance and church societies, there are the St. Patrick's, St. George's and Highland Societies, organized for benevolent purposes.

The County Poor House, situated at the upper end of the town, is a large building governed by a Board of Commissioners appointed by the county. The management is said to be excellent, each town paying its ratio of expenses for its own poor, besides a proportionate share for current expenses. At the time of my visit there were only ten occupants in the building, mostly aged persons, and not one of those came from Chatham.

The Chatham police force consists of but three men, whose services are not often required. There are no water works, but the town is well supplied with water from numerous springs, and several large tanks are placed at convenient distances for fire purposes.

The fire department is a volunteer organization. There is one steam engine, two hand engines, and one chemical extinguisher. A fire broke out during my short stay, and I had the opportunity of seeing the men turned out on short notice. This is the first town east of Rivière du Loup, that has an organized fire department. It is really extraordinary to find the apathy with which the people of other places regard the possible contingency of fire. In small towns, completely shut out from aid, should a conflagration occur, there could be no possible means of escape from the disastrous losses which would most asuredly follow without the aid of proper apparatus. The lesson taught by the fire at St. John's seems to be wholly lost on the inhabitants of remote country places. When you do come across a hand engine it is generally in a state of mechanical bankruptcy—completely useless. While upon this subject, I may add that evidences of the great Miramichi fire of 1825, already referred to, are still to be seen along the North Shore by the dead trees which lie extended in one direction through the burnt woods.

COMMERCIAL.

Chatham does not bear any evidence of the "commercial depression." The phrase seems to be unknown here. There is plenty of work to be had, and poverty, as it is understood in Montreal, is unknown. When I began to speak of the check which our trade had received, and the continued depressed state of the industries of the country, people began to regard me as a sort of paid commissioner sent to Chatham to make out a case against the Government. Said a man to me, whose ignorance of politics was exceedingly amusing :—"We have *no* depression, sir; Chatham is GREATLY BLESSED, sir. Indeed it is HIGHLY FAVORED, sir. We have no politics, and, sir, I am glad to say we have no politicians, and that's the reason, *I guess, why we haven't got any commercial depression, sir.* No, sir, the only depression we experience in Chatham, sir, is we're getting down-hearted because we can't get men to turn out work fast enough, sir. Yes, sir, Chatham is the metropolis of the North Shore, and if you want to settle down here, sir, this is the place to settle in." Having said this, the Chatham man looked at me defiantly, and walked off. His view of the subject, however, is scarcely exaggerated; the people are industrious and happy-looking. The staple produce is lumber.

THE LUMBER TRADE

affords employment to at least 600 persons. There are five mills in the town and three in the vicinity. One of these employs three gangs of men by day, cutting from 150,000 to 175,000 feet in ten hours; also two gangs by night, cutting from 100,000 to 120,000 in the same time. In this mill alone 240 men are employed. Here the logs are taken out of the water in the tree, passed through the mill, sawn, and in *one minute and a half* (by checked time) the planks are placed in the vessel and ready for the foreign market. At the wharf of this mill, seven vessels, averaging 500 tons each, were being loaded as fast as possible. This fine mill is the property of Mr. J. B. Snowball. The Hon. Wm. Muirhead owns the oldest saw-mill on the Miramichi, originally built by Joseph Cunard, about the year 1835.

The wages of the men who are employed at or about the mills varies from $1.25 to $2.50 per day. Most of the operatives own the houses in which they live, and not a few of them possess other property.

The following

TABLE OF EXPORTS FOR 1876, ENDING JUNE 30TH,

represents the quantity and value of this large industry :—

DEALS AND BOARDS.

Countries.	Quantity.	Value.
United Kingdom....................	88,200,000 feet.	$905,393
France	1,157,000 "	11,573
Holland	782,000 "	8,590
St. Pierre	318,000 "	2,377
	90,457,000 feet.	$927,933

DEAL ENDS.

United Kingdom....................	3,720,000 feet.	$ 27,439
France	51,000 "	365
Holland	29,000 "	204
	3,800,000 feet.	$ 28,008

SCANTLING.

United Kingdom	2,969,000 feet.	$ 22,552

TIMBER—PINE.

United Kingdom	1,853 tons.	$ 14,255

TIMBER—BIRCH.

United Kingdom	817 tons.	$ 5,656
France	31 "	155
	848 tons.	$ 5,811

PALINGS.

United Kingdom	2,543,000 pieces.	$ 12,163

SPARS.

France.......................Number........ 44		$ 176

During the same period the imports were valued at $114,535; consumption at $132,337, and the amount of duty paid to the Government, $29,565.30

THE FISHERY QUESTION ONCE MORE.

There are three canning establishments within easy distance of Chatham, viz., at Fox Island, Miramichi Bay, and Burnt Church, on the north side, 24 miles distant. Large quantities are exported to England, and also packed in ice and sent by rail to Boston and New York.

The official returns for 1876 show the following fish exports :—

	Pounds.	Value.
Lobsters (canned) United Kingdom..............	273,120	$21,963
Salmon, do. do.	49,698	6,801
	Barrels.	
Pickled fish, United States....................	1,199	4,297
Total value		$33,075

In addition to its lumber and fishing trade, Chatham has two steam tanneries and two large iron foundries.

An extensive trade is also carried on between here and Prince Edward Island. Oats, potatoes and other **farm produce** are taken in exchange for lumber and manufactured goods.

In remarking upon the shipping of **Chatham**, it should be mentioned that two-thirds **of** the vessels named below were loading at the time of my visit.

LIST OF VESSELS IN PORT AUGUST 6TH, 1876.

Owners.		tons.
Wm. Muirhead	1 ship	1049
"	8 barques	4189
"	1 barquentine	395
"	1 brig	293
"	1 schooner	585
Total. 12		6511
J. B. Snowball	1 ship	681
"	6 barques	3711
"	2 brigs	713
"	1 barquentine	220
Total 10		5325
George Stewart & Co	1 barque	353
"	1 brig	318
Total 2		671
A. M. Morrison	2 barques	869
"	1 brig	220
"	1 brigantine	229
Total 4		1318

	Vessels.	Tonnage.
Wm. Muirhead	12	6511
J. B. Snowball	10	5325
George Stewart & Co	2	671
A. Morrison	4	1318
Total	28	13825

All trading.

Besides these there were **28 other vessels loading** and unloading, **viz.,** 12 British, 7 Norwegian, 4 **German**, 2 **United States**, 2 Russian **and** 1 Austrian.

You will admit this is an important exhibit for a town of **4,000** persons.

POINTS OF INTEREST.

The country surrounding Chatham is generally level **and has** an agricultural district extending from **one to nine miles out of town. Nine miles,** south, you strike Black River, the settlements along which extend about five miles, and easterly thirteen miles, where the river empties into Miramichi Bay. Good trout fishing may be had at Tubusciatic and at Burnt Church River, which empties into Miramichi Bay, below Chatham. Abundance of wild fowl may be shot in the spring and fall. Cariboo and moose hunting is carried on extersively in mid-winter, but shooting is not permitted after February 1st. They may be found in the direction of Bartibogue river, a tributary of the Miramichi, and at Point Escuminiac, the southern entrance to the Bay. The Marine Hospital at Douglastown (a settlement between Chatham and Newcastle) is a stone edifice, and is said to be well adapted for the purpose. Douglastown was formerly known as the centre of extensive milling operations.

RAILROAD FREIGHTS

are said to give general satisfaction here. Flour is brought from Toronto for $55 per 100 barrels, and by steamer for $75 for the same quantity. While upon the subject of transportation, let me tell you something of the

CHATHAM BRANCH RAILWAY,

which connects with the Intercolonial at Chatham Junction. The road is eight miles long, and cost $70,000. It was opened July 25th, and is not yet complete, though it connects with the day mail from Quebec. There is no doubt that it will ultimately prove a paying concern, and it shows that the Chatham people are fully alive to the great value which the Intercolonial will be to them. The line passes through rich farm lands, crossing the highroads diagonally. The crops look in excellent condition and the land is well tilled. The produce is principally oats, barley, wheat, potatoes and other roots. Some very fine cattle and horses from imported stock are owned by well-to-do farmers. Some have recently been brought here from Prince Edward Island, and are in first-class condition.

Chatham is not only well favored, abundantly blessed and evidently prosperous, but it is far ahead of any other town, for its size, in the Maritime Provinces.

No. X.

FROM CHATHAM JUNCTION TO MONCTON.

Again I shall have to try the reader's patience by a dry recital of hard facts. The beautiful scenery; the picturesque attractions of lake, river, mountain and sky; of fields of heather, of forests of pine; of fishing, and of traditional historic interest—these attractions are left far behind, and I must again settle myself down to matters of commonplace description which, however, must not be ommitted in the geneal record of the trip.

THE BRIDGES OVER THE MIRAMICHI.

The description of the line would not be complete without some reference to the superb samples of railroad engineering in connection with the bridges of the Miramichi and Restigouche. They were erected by Messrs Clark, Reeves & Co., of Philadelphia, and are known as the Pratt Truss. The difficulties which had to be surmounted were of a nature requiring the skill of the ablest engineers.

The one crossing the South-West branch was commenced in May, 1871 and opened by Sir W. O'Grady Haley on the 28th August, 1875. The total length is 1,244 feet, of six spans, approached by an embankment three hundred feet in length, extending beyond the river bank, thus making the total width of the river crossing nearly 1,550 feet. Before this could be built gigantic preliminary difficulties were encountered, as for instance the excavation, pumping, &c., previous to sinking the caissons thirty-five feet below the river's bed. Nearly seven hundred yards of excavation were required for each pier. These caissons were built of twelve-inch lumber, filled with concrete, seventy-three feet long, twenty-five feet broad and thirty-five feet deep, and are sunk to their entire depth in the gravelly soil. These caissons form the foundations of the piers. Upon the top of the caissons the masonry is built, covering the same plane area as the caissons On the up-stream side are cutwaters, faced with granite, rising twenty fee from the beginning of the masonry. The tops of the cutwaters have a flat surface fifteen feet square. These are built to avoid the ice jams which might otherwise affect the structure. The piers contain seven hundred and forty yards of masonry and are twenty-nine feet by ten at the top. The stones used in building the piers range in courses, each stone being from two feet, six inches at the bottom, to one foot three inches at the top. The masonry is laid with Portland cement of the best quality. Thirteen thousand barrels were used on this and on the North-West bridge, to which reference will be made directly. Little or no vibration is felt beyond the slight rumbling sound caused by the sleepers. The abutments contain 1200 cubic yards of masonry. Each abutment is forty feet long by twenty-nine feet extreme width. The superstructures of bridges of this kind were previously built of wood, but it was thought better to use iron in this instance. The truss work is eighty feet high and eighteen feet wide. The design of the " Pratt Truss" somewhat resembles an inverted hopper. Its merit may be said to lie in the fact that the weight of the different portions of the iron-work is relieved by the arrangement of the cross beams and railings, by which the strain bears equally upon each part, and the whole is reduced to a minimum. Each span is a little over one hundred tons in weight. The bridge is painted white, not only to give it a light appearance, but for the easier detection of rust.

The North-West bridge differs only from the former in regard to the foundation. This bridge was begun in 1872 and completed in September, 1875. The caissons in this instance are " open." They are sunk to the bed of the river and surrounded by sheet piling, **driven fast to the gravel bed at an** average distance of fifty feet below high water. The caissons are sixty feet long and thirty feet wide. The **cutwaters have no** tables as in the South-west bridge. The top of the **masonry above the** highest spring tides is about twenty-five feet. The cost **of these bridges is esti-** mated at *one million dollars!*

The gentlemen **who assisted to construct these monuments of scientific** triumph—for **they may well be regarded as such—are Mr. Peter Grant,** C. E., who **designed the plans; Mr. A. S. Brown, of Messrs. Brown & Co., of** Belleville, Ont., who **personally supervised the construction; Mr. W. E.** Smellie, Superintending Engineer, **and Mr. W. W. Lee, Managing Mechani-** cal **Engineer.**

The description which **I have attempted falls far short** of the true impression of admiration which these mammoth structures are calculated to inspire those who are familiar with all the **details of** engineering science. But I had

A NARROW ESCAPE

from a fearful infliction of **enthusiasm on the** part of a tourist whose ideas of poetry and science were very much mixed. The young gentleman finding that I was connected **with the Fourth Estate,** improvised an elegant tribute to "Science in the forest lonely," in which he, with the very best intentions in the world, **intended to convey a delicate compliment** to the enterprise of the GAZETTE in furnishing the public with an account of "A Trip over the Intercolonial." He button-holed me with three samples of machine poetry, which, measured by the foot, would have occupied about a column of your journal. His **facility for rhyming was** extraordinary; his love of the beautiful **was in proportion to his rhyme;** but his composition lacked two important features—**brevity and** common sense. His indulgence in poetic license positively **amounted to literary libertinism.** With a pleading and almost a fearful face, he **begged my acceptance of** what he considered to be the **best of his compositions. I give you two** verses, because I should not like to discourage native talent even in its most crude form. This is what he has handed down to posterity :—

"THE POET'S TRIBUTE TO SCIENCE."

"Ye bridges who span Miramichi's fairest waters,
　With iron-girt bands in this wild forest, lone;
A tribute of science to our sons and our daughters,
　Where skill hath erected a home of its own.
The forest trees murmur in deep tribulation;
　The beaver and moose retreat as in fear,
While the Iron King's shriek brings news that a nation
　Has conquered the forest, the river, and deer.

What a good **thing it is for editors that men of genius like this** sometimes take a holiday.

There are yet eight railway stations to be disposed of before Moncton is reached.

Chatham Junction is 123 feet above sea level. The station is 302 miles from Riviere du Loup. Four miles from it is Barnaby River station, at an elevation of but forty-nine feet. A quarter mile east of it and over the first crossing of Barnaby River is a lattice girder bridge 100 feet long. The land retains the same uninteresting appearance as noted in my last letter. Four miles east of Barnaby River station and over the second crossing of the river is another bridge with a single span of eighty feet. The soil is about six feet deep, when you find freestone rock of good quality and of which the masonry is composed.

The next station is Forest, 298 feet above sea level. Nine miles further you reach

Ferris station, 257 feet above the sea. One mile east of Ferris a bridge with a single span of eighty feet crosses the Kouchibouguacis River. The land here is only remarkable for its almost utter worthlessness. This portion of the line is on Section 21, beginning one mile west of the river, and extending one and three-quarter miles east of the Miramichi. The section contains 140,000 cubic yards of rock cutting, 7,000 yards of earth and 8,000 yards of masonry. A culvert fifteen feet long spans the fifth crossing of the Barnaby River. One mile beyond the fourth crossing the river flows through a tunnel twenty feet square, cut through solid sandstone for a distance of 110 feet. The gap is filled up with an embankment. The course of the River Kouchibouguacis by means of a segmental arch thirty feet long. This arch is cut through an embankment of 150,000 cubic yards of earth. It is 1,500 feet long and sixty feet high.

Eleven miles distant from Truro is

Welford Station, at an elevation of 193 feet above the sea. Two miles west of here a single span bridge eighty feet long crosses the Richibucto River. From its central situation, it is thought that Weldford will be an important station.

Coal Branch Station, nine miles east, is 203 feet above sea level. A bridge of three spans, each forty feet long crosses the

COAL BRANCH RIVER.

Each bridge is forty-two feet above the river. On the east side of the station is another of three spans of forty feet each. The river is a tributary of the Richibucto, and small quantities of coal are found along its stream. Five miles east of Coal Branch River, a bridge of thirty spans crosses the Buctouche River.

The next station, nine miles distant, is Canaan, 156 feet above the sea It is crossed by a ten foot arched culvert The country is boggy and great difficulty was experienced in poling and brushing the road through which the line passes. Four miles east of Canaan River is a bridge of a single span of twenty-four feet. Five miles east of the station is a second bridge over the South Cocaigne River of a single span of twenty-four feet.

This is the last bridge along the line before reaching Moncton.

On following page you will find

A LIST of all the BRIDGES between RIVIERE DU LOUP and MONCTON.

Distance from Rivière du Loup	LOCATION.	No. of Spans.	Total length in feet
Miles.			
0	Rivière du Loup...........................	3	300
17½	½ mile west of Isle Verte.................	2	160
27	Trois Pistoles............................	5	500
47½	½ mile east of St. Fabian Station, over Grand Bic River..	1	80
55	Bic Station, over Little Bic River............	1	110
66½	½ mile west of Rimouski Station, over Rimouski River....	5	240
88	4 miles east of St. Flavie, over Metis River............	4	400
105	2 miles east of Tartague, over Tartague River..........	1	50
112½	½ mile west of Sayabec, over Sayabec River............	1	24
114	1 mile east of Sayabec, over St. Pierre River...........	1	80
124	4 miles east of Cedar Hall Station, over Tobago River ...	1	30
128½	½ mile east of Amqui Station, over Amqui River........	1	100
136	2 miles east of Amqui Station, over Indian Brook.......	3	150
141	At Causaposcal Station, over Metapedia River	3	300
146	5 miles east of Causaposcal, over Metapedia River.......	3	300
160	4 miles east of Assametquaghan, over McKinnon's Brook.	3	180
164	2 miles west of Mill Stream Station, over Metapedia River	4	400
176	At Metapedia Station, over Restigouche River..........	5	1000
183	7 miles east of Metapedia Station, over Christopher's Brook	7	420
190	1 mile east of Campbellton Station, over Mill Creek.....	3	180
203	5 miles east of Dalhousie Station, over Eel River........	1	100
209	1 mile east of Charlo Station, over north branch of Charlo R.	3	150
	Within 300 feet of south branch of Charlo River........	2	100
214½	½ mile east of New Mills, over Benjamin River..........	2	120
220	6 miles east of New Mills, over Nash's Creek..........	1	80
221	7 miles east of New Mills, over Louison's Brook........	1	60
222	1 mile west of Jacquet River, and crossing it...........	3	300
227	4 miles east of Jacquet River, crossing Belledune River..	1	80
238	2 miles east of Petit Roche, over Elm Tree River........	1	80
243	3 miles east of Petit Roche, over Nigados River.........	1	80
249	3 miles west of Bathurst, Tete-à-Gauche	5	500
254	2 miles east of Bathurst Station, over Middle River......	2	160
255	3 miles east of Bathurst, over Little River.............	1	60
257	5 miles east of Bathurst, crossing Nipisiguit River.......	6	600
260	5 miles west of Red Pine Station, over Red Pine Brook ..	3	120
279	4 miles east of Bartibogue Station, over Bartibogue River	1	80
299	3 miles east of Miramichi, over North West Branch	6	1200
299½	½ mile from the above, and over the South West Branch..	6	1200
306½	½ mile east of Barnaby Sta'n, over first crossing of Barnaby R.	1	100
310	4 miles " " " second " "	1	80
314	8 miles east of Barnaby Station, over the third crossing of Barnaby River.................................	1	80
327	1 mile east of Ferris Station, near Kouchibouguacis River.	1	80
335	2 miles west of Weldford, over Richibucto River........	1	80
346	At Coal Branch Station, over the North Coal Brook	3	120
	Over S. Branch of the Coal Branch on east side of station.	3	120
351	5 miles east of Coal Branch, near the Buctouche River. ..	1	30
359	4 miles east of Canaan, over North Cocaigne River......	1	24
363	3 miles west of Berry's Mills, over North River.........	1	50
	Total length, feet		10838

4

The amount of money which these forty-eight bridges cost, I have not been able to ascertain. It is probable that even the Hon. the Minister of Public Works has not yet completed his returns concerning them.

It should be mentioned that all those bridges over fifty feet span are the lattice girder. Those within that length are of the ordinary plate girder construction. The difference is this : the former rest upon expansion rollers to allow for construction and expansion, but no such provision is considered necessary for the plate girder bridge. There are only two wooden bridges along the line and these are at Riviere du Loup and Trois Pistoles. A contractor informed me that 75,000 yards of track between Campbelton and Moncton have yet to be ballasted before the road can be said to be thoroughly completed in this particular.

Berry's Mills is the next station which you pass; it is 208 feet above sea level. Between here and Moncton the track is almost a straight line, and continues for thirty-one miles from the former station. None of the curves are greater than 2 ° 30" with the exception of a 4 ° 30" curve just before you reach Moncton. Some of them even vary from $\frac{1}{2}$° to 1 ° 30". The grade is exceedingly smooth, and standing on the platform of the last car, the train going at a speed of forty miles per hour, the beauty of the line is exceedingly pleasing to the eye.

As I cannot tell you much about the scenery between Miramichi and Moncton (because I defy the greatest lover of nature to get up an enthusiasm about it), perhaps I may be able to tell you something about the way in which the country has been "cut up" along the line. The first section from Moncton is 23. It terminates at a short distance west of Buctouche. The amount of masonry is 3,980 yards of the first class, and 1,630 of the second class. There are 31,000 cubic yards of rock cutting and 624 cubic yards of earth. A short distance east of Berry's Mills, at Jonathan Creek, is an embankment containing 150,000 cubic yards of earth. Near Berry's Mills, and east of the track, is the Lutz Mountain settlement, containing a population of 300. On the west is Steves Mountain settlement, whose inhabitants chiefly grow potatoes, hay, oats and buckwheat. There is also a fair sprinkling of good lumber in the vicinity. West of here the track curves around the point of Indian Mountain by a half degree curve 1$\frac{1}{2}$ miles in radius.

Nine miles from Berry's Station you reach Moncton, being a distance of 374 miles from Riviere du Loup.

No. XI.

MONCTON.

This is the eastern terminus of the Northern Division of the Intercolonial. The station is about 42 feet above sea level. Before going into a description of the general offices, car shops, etc., of the line it would be well perhaps to say something of the town itself.

THE TOWN

contains a population of about 4,000, and is built on the bend of the Peticodiac. This river is remarkable for the rapidity with which the tide ebbs
and flows. As the tide rushes along it forms a "bore" or wall of water,
making a breastwork, as it were, across the channel. The sight of this
immense body of water has induced persons from long distances to visit
the singular phenomenon. This "wall" commences at Stony Creek,
seven miles distant, and travels at the rate of seven miles per hour with
the flood tide.

The streets of Moncton are well laid out, although the houses are somewhat scattered. The town contains seven churches. There are two
factories in Moncton; the first, an iron foundry, owned by Mr. C. B.
Record, covers two and a half acres of ground and gives employment to
thirty-five men. The factory appears to be thoroughly well fitted in its
various departments, which include the moulding shop, the fitting shop,
blacksmiths', pattern and machine shops, in addition to a separate department for the manufacture of ploughs, which have gained some celebrity
throughout the Province. The other establishment is a soap factory,
owned by Mr. Torrie.

Moncton is well provided with

SCHOOLS.

One large building contains seven schools, and three other edifices are
in course of construction. The whole, when finished, will cost about
$20,000, exclusive of an annual expense to the people of the town of $3000
apart from county and Government aid.

From its central position Moncton is bound to come into prominence.
Already two bank branches are doing a fair business. The one is the bank
of Montreal, the other the Bank of British North America.

There is good wharfage here, and would make a capital place for shipbuilding and lumber business, both of which industries have fallen off of
late. The question of building a dry dock at Moncton has been revived
from time to time ; but it is questionable whether it will be put into practical shape for some time to come. Whether it would benefit the town or
not yet remains an open question.

THE SURROUNDING COUNTRY

is devoted to farming. The crops are well forward. Crossing the river
Peticodiac is a wooden bridge 1,700 feet long, which costs $80,000. This
bridge connects with the county of Albert, which has a population of 10,000.
The county is rich in its mineral resources, and is the seat of the celebrated Albert Mine, which has gained a reputation for the bituminous quality
of its coal.

A branch railway has been built from Salisbury, fifteen miles above
Moncton, to Hopewell's Corner, forty miles long.

Twenty miles from here is Dorchester, the shire town of the county

(Westmoreland), where the new Penitentiary for the Maritime Provinces is about to be built. This edifice, it is said, will cost $500,000, but this would appear to be an exaggerated estimate.

Moncton, which was only incorporated last year, is governed by a town council of six members, who elect their own chairman. Two men constitute the police force. Robberies occasionally occur, and, for a place of its size, two men are not enough. There is also a fire company, and an excellent new engine, purchased last year.

A weekly paper, the Moncton *Times*, is published in the Conservative interest.

THE WORKING FORCE OF THE LINE FROM RIVIÈRE DU LOUP TO HALIFAX.

From figures which have been furnished me here I have compiled the following approximate table of weekly expenditure for wages alone. As I could not get full particulars, on account of the absence of some of the officials, the following statement must be taken as far below the actual cost of working the road, for it will be observed that it does not include the salaries of the highest officers. It is merely given to enable the reader to form an approximate idea of the cost for labor only :—

Number of Employes.	NATURE OF DUTY.	Average Daily Wages.	Average Weekly Wages.
		$ c.	$ c.
700	Shopmen.		
670	Engineers.		
	This number includes other employés in locomotive and car shops. The rate of wages of these men is from $1.30 to $2.20. Placing it an average of $1.75 per day, it would represent for 1,370 men a daily expenditure amounting to..............................	2,397 50	14,385.00
900	Trackmen at $1.10 per day................	990.00	5,940.00
400	Station men whose average wages are $500 per year, or per week $9.62. This for 400 men would give	....	3,848.00
340	Trainmen, including conductors, at $2.21 per day, and brakesmen at $1.35 per day......		
	Say 75 conductors at $2.21 per day..........	165.75	994.50
	Say 265 brakesmen at $1.35 per day.........	357.75	2,146.50
56	Officers and clerks.		
	Say 16 officers at an average salary of $1,000 per year ; or per week, each, $19.23 ; or for the 16 a total of	....	307.68
	Say 40 clerks at an average of $600 per year ; or per week, each, of $11.53, representing, for the 40	....	461.20
3,066	Employés represent a total weekly expenditure of	....	28,082.88

RECEIPTS FROM THE ROAD.

I was much disappointed at not being able to get a copy of the Returns of the Traffic Receipts since the opening of the line, which I was informed had not yet been made public. The only information I could get on this point was that the receipts from traffic since July 1st had been, in round figures, about $100,000 per month. That the bulk of the traffic was between Campbellton and St. John, of which fully seventy per cent. was between St. John and Moncton.

THE WORKSHOPS.

The shops, though large and roomy, are certainly not elaborate. There is nothing superfluous or costly about them. Cleanliness and discipline were very noticeable. There are about four hundred men engaged here in the various departments. The shops include the machine, erecting, blacksmiths', boiler, tinsmiths', carpenter, paint and pattern-maker's shops, beside the brass foundry. The machine and blacksmiths' shop alone cover an acre of ground. An excellent provision is made in case of fire by means of Knowles' steam pump, made in Boston, which has a capacity of throwing 1,000 gallons per minute. There are three car shops, the first is two hundred and seventy-six by seventy-six feet, the second three hundred by forty-five feet, and the third one hundred and seventy-five by forty feet. At the time of my visit there were two hundred freight cars in course of construction besides twenty others, including passenger, express, smoking and conductors' cars. There is a peculiarity in connection with the latter which should be mentioned. There are twelve built, thirty feet long, and ten feet wide, with a " bulge " or bow window in the side extending from the body of the car, by which means the conductors can have an uninterrupted view of the whole train before and behind. It was originally suggested to place an elevated seat for this purpose above the roof of the car, (as is the case in some of the cars in the United States) but for some reason or another this idea was abandoned. I believe the present plan is designed by Mr. Robt. Luttrell. The workshops are substantially built of brick, and to describe properly would take at least two columns of your journal. It took me an hour and a half to go through the various mechanical departments, only casually noting the various objects of interest. Any description I would give you would be necessarily dry and perhaps uninteresting to the general reader.

THE GENERAL OFFICES

are in a large, handsome brick building, and are elaborately fitted with the most improved office furniture and latest telegraphic improvements. The building is the headquarters for the General Superintendent, the Paymaster, the Engineer, Accountant, and Storekeeper.

is an exceedingly handsome building, to which is attached a dining saloon said to be the finest in the Dominion. In the station is the General Passenger Agent's office and Baggage Master's Department.

This letter concludes the full description of the Northern Division of the Intercolonial Railway, in the completion of which your correspondent is much indebted to the officers, employees and private individuals along the line, who have invariably given him every reasonable information they have been able to impart.

No. XII.

ST. JOHN, N. B.

So far as the construction of the Intercolonial Railway is concerned, there is little, if anything, to add to what has already been mentioned To those who may not be familiar with the official divisions of the line it may be said that St. John is one of the termini of the Western Division, of which Amherst, N. S., is the eastern terminus. The distance from Moncton is eighty-nine miles, and from Riviere du Loup it is four hundred and sixty-three miles. The country between Amherst and St. John is agricultural; passing the stations of Sackville, Dorchester, Moncton, Salisbury, Sussex, Hampton, and Rothesay, in addition to smaller villages, which it is not necessary to describe here.

This division is not a new one, and it would be impossible in the general features of these letters to observe the same completeness of detail which has hitherto been followed out. And for a good reason; the monotony of description would soon weary the reader. However, the more noteworthy places between St. John and Moncton will be dealt with in another form.

With regard to St. John, there is so much to be said and written about it that one is almost at a loss to know where to begin. To go back to 1604, when the first French ship sailed into its harbor on the 24th of June, down to the present date, would require the gift of an historian to present the details in their proper form. I cannot give any better reference to its historical and commercial associations than to advise the reader to peruse an excellent little work entitled "St. John and its Business," compiled by Mr. G. A. White. It contains everything of general interest from 1604 to 1850, and as a reference book it is handy and reliable.

The St. John of to-day is a strange mixture of rocks and water, of magnificence and squalor. The difficulties of building and improving the city have been and are still enormous, and speak well for the energy and indomitable pluck of the builders. Without intending to be profane, it may be truthfully asserted that St. John is emphatically a "blasted city."

But the hopes of its people are as bright and cheerful as their hearts and manners are warm and hospitable. If you want gas in your house, you must cut through rock to lay your pipe. It will cost you a small fortune to do this. If you want water you must do likewise. In fact, if you want anything in the way of street improvents, you are met with difficult-ies at almost every turn. The result is that taxes are about as high as they can go. But St. John folk are a patient people. They always mur-mur inwardly ; and never seem to care about knowing on what basis assessments are made. For instance : a clerk with a salary of $600 per year is taxed on his personal income at thirteen dollars ; another with the same salary has to pay twenty dollars. Why this difference exists is an enigma which no one can explain with any degree of satisfaction. The people grumble occasionally at mismanagement ; but it never amounts to anything. Once in a while a liberal-hearted citizen will pray for an in-junction to restrain the payment of salaries to Aldermen, and defray the law costs out of his own pocket. The people let him do it and nobody seems to mind it, except a few of the Aldermen, and even they admire, in spite of themselves, the public spirit which prompts the action. The commercial part of the town occupies about a square mile. The offices along the market square are, with a few exceptions, dingy, wooden structures ; but they contain the records of owners of fleets of vessels which carry traffic to all parts of the world. Water street, a thoroughfare running north and south, parallel to the har-bor, is full of red brick blocks, not unlike some of the back streets of Liverpool. But there is a business-like air about the street which pos-sesses a sort of attraction. True, there isn't much splendor worth speaking of ; but then these blocks were not built for ornament, but for use. They have served their purpose, and their owners have grown rich. The wharves in many places sadly need repairing, and they are in general keeping with the offices around them. The forests of masts standing out boldly in the harbor, as seen from Fort Howe, a dismantled fort in the town of Portland, adjoining the city, and northwest of the same, is a sight worth seeing. You have nothing in Montreal to excel it in interest and diversity of landscape. Partridge Island, with its lighthouse, two and a half miles from the city ; the Suspension Bridge ; Indiantown, a portion of Portland ; and the bold, broad sweep of water, on a clear day (which has been rare lately), form one magnificent stretch of scenery, full of attraction and interest to the observer.

The suburbs of St. John, whose interests are identical with the city, are Carleton on the west side of the harbor, which was incorporated with the city a few years ago, and Portland on the east side. The latter is control-led by a town council, whose proceedings are usually characterized by much oracular force, but very little executive ability. The rate-payers have lately reduced the salary of their magistrate owing to the reduction in the receipts of that portion of the municipal revenue derived from po-lice court fines. Whether this is an implied censure on the ability of that excellent official I cannot say; but judging from the report of the proceedings of the Portland Town Council published in the city newspapers one would imagine that because the fines are becoming fewer, the salary of the magistrate should also become reduced in a like ratio. This is one view of justice which will possess the appearance of novelty to Montrealers.

The streets in the city of St. John are built at right angles; but it would be more correct to say they are mostly rectangular curves. Very few of them are level, owing to the rocky nature of the soil and the difficulty of grading. The two principal thoroughfares are Prince William street and King street. The former runs north and south; the latter from west to east. The appearance of the city from the Market Square is very imposing. Both the above streets are broad, well paved and well lighted. The shops are very handsome, and the windows are dressed with taste and skill. The lamplighters of St. John, however, by a strange oversight peculiar to those gentlemen, and not alone confined to St. John, often manage to brilliantly light up the thoroughfares to shame the moon on pleasant evenings, and on dark nights they leave the city in Egyptian gloom. This is supposed to arise from economical principles, but the error may be attributed to incorrect information obtained from old almanacs; however, the facts remain the same. The west side of the harbor has no gas. But it has very bad sidewalks, and between the one and the other the result is a serious accident now and then; a law suit for damages; heavy compensation; and thus the "penny wise and pound foolish policy" works admirably. Carleton people want all the improvements which the eastern part of the city possesses, but do not want to pay for them. There is much human nature in Carleton in this respect.

The principal thoroughfares in St. John, other than those already mentioned, are Germain street, running parallel with Prince William street; City road, on the north, and Main street on the south. Charlotte, Waterloo and Brussels streets are also worthy of mention.

One of the sights of St. John is

KING STREET ON SATURDAY NIGHT.

Then the excellent asphalt sidewalks are thronged with thousands of pedestrians, of all sizes, shades and colors. At the head of King street is a wooden archway, with a bell tower—more useful than ornamental. The archway is so mellowed by time that at a distance it looks like stone. The design is graceful, but the fraud on the stone is very apparent when you come to examine it. Stretching across the roadway, on both sides of Charlotte street for a distance of 300 or 400 yards, you find a procession of idlers, with their hands in their pockets, helping the policemen to keep the peace. In fact, you can scarcely tell the policemen from the lookers-on. There they stand, gazing on the passing multitude, jesting, laughing, cursing and swearing, with the air of millionaires. This chronic habit of street-corner loafing is peculiar to St. John. A few young men, with

nothing to do, appropriate the lease of a street corner, and stay there till midnight. It doesn't matter whether it rains or shines, you will be almost sure to find the same faces at the same corners; unconsciously trying to rub smooth the lamp posts and store corners with their shoulders. They appear to appropriate their special *rendezvous* with the same right as a crossing-sweeper appropriates a crossing. No matter to what part of the city you may go, reputable or disreputable, you will invariably find the street lounger at his post. What they do or how they live is a mystery. But they appear to live well, and are kept busy—loafing.

The archway referred to is at the head of King square, which would make a capital garden if a little more attention was paid to it. This is a popular resort for itinerant preachers, where religion becomes a hollow mockery by the jest and gibes of those who go to scoff and remain to ridicule. The Christianizing influences of religion are here a mere burlesque, made so, unwittingly, by amateur theologians whose knowledge of doctrine is as limited as their knowledge of grammar.

King street, East, a continuation of King square, contains some fine private residences. Queen square is also another popular resort. It is a few blocks south of the former. It is by far the superior of the two, but, like the former, could be considerably improved.

But St. John possesses other attractions of a more substantial nature in keeping with its enterprise and thrift.

PRINCIPAL BUILDINGS.

First in point of beauty is the city Post Office on Prince William street, erected at a cost of $200,000. Its dimensions are ninety and fifty feet, built of stone. The style of architecture is modern. The front is really superb, fully equal to any building of the size in Montreal. Each side of, and over the entrance are sixteen red, polished, Bay of Fundy granite columns, the beauty of which excites general admiration. The roof is a mansard, surmounted by a graceful tower, from which an exquisite view of many miles can be had. This fine office has every facility for the prompt assortment and delivery of the mails.

Next comes the

NEW CITY MARKET.

This fine brick structure occupies a block nearly four hundred feet long and eighty feet wide. Its western end faces Germain street, and the eastern, Charlotte. There are two streets running parallel with and at each side of the building. This handsome structure cost $150,000, and it is mainly due to the energy of the popular Mayor, Chipman Smith, Esq., that the building was erected. It would pay the City Council of Montreal to send a commissioner here to take a few lessons in the art of building a market. The floor is of asphalt, at a grade of fifteen feet. It has 1,500 feet of stand accommodation. Every stall is thoroughly and neatly fitted with

good cellarage and ample water supply. The money was raised in debentures, which have forty years to run. It is expected that after paying the
interest on these debentures there will be a surplus left to retire them, so
that, eventually, the city will have a market of its own, free of debt, and
from which at least $10,000 per year will be realized.

In the western end of the building is a hall eighty by fifty feet, surrounded by a gallery twelve feet wide, the height of the ceiling being twenty-
four feet. This hall is admirably suited for a

FREE PUBLIC LIBRARY,

and I understand the City Council has, at the request of many influential
citizens, expressed its willingness to hand it over for that purpose. The
immense advantage which this would be to the public is apparent. St.
John, a city of so much importance to the Maritime Provinces, will doubtless secure this long-felt want at an early day. I might tell you, if I had
time, of the fine Roman Catholic Cathedral on Waterloo street, built of
stone, and as perfect a specimen of Gothic architecture as any I have seen.
Or I might dilate on the Wiggins' Male Orphan Asylum, another handsome
red brick edifice, four stories high. This is on Brittain street, and was
erected at the private cost of the late Stephen Wiggins, Esq., merchant
and shipowner. Then I could ask you to accompany me to the Maritime
Bank, about which so much has been said of late ; an elegant stone building on the south-east corner of Market square. From there you can take
the ferry at Water street, cross over to Carleton and view the Albert School
building. We have no public school building to surpass it Montreal ; in
fact it is the redeeming feature of Carleton. While here, it would be well
to take a look at the suspension bridge, crossing the Falls of the St. John
River. It well repays a visit. This elegant bridge, six hundred and four
feet long, is one hundred feet above low water. It was built and projected
by W. K. Reynolds, Esq., of Lepreaux, and cost $80,000. It was finished
in 1853, and on the 1st of July, 1874, the Provincial Government bought
it and made it a free highway. Suppose we cross it ; take a glance
up and down the river, inhale for a moment the fresh sea breeze
coming from the south, and look in for a moment on Dr. Sleeves,
the physician of the Provincial Lunatic Asylum. He will tell
you that the fine red brick institution, with the extensive farm, gardens,
and shrubberies, is not large enough to accommodate the number of unfortunate creatures who seek a home within its walls. Its ample corridors,
neat rooms, and generally clean appearance, do not, however, relieve you
of the feeling of sadness which creeps over you at the sight of such mental prostration. Suppose, then, we leave it, not forgetting to contribute
our mite towards alleviating the wants of these poor people. Let us re-
trace our steps, wend our way to Carleton, and take the ferry to St. John.
Half an hour will bring us to where we started, and if you feel tired we
will take a carriage by the hour and "do" the remaining buildings of

note. After glancing at the granite-faced **Custom House, a substantial building** some 300 feet long, facing **on** Prince **William street, it would not be a bad** idea to drive **to** the Victoria Hotel, **at the corner of Duke and** Germain streets, **and partake of a** glass of **claret with mine host Swett. He** will take you **over one of the finest** hotels in **the Dominion, which occupies over 100 feet square. The hall alone is** 40 x 20 **feet, and the vestibule** 20 **x 15 feet, the floors of which are inlaid with marble. The dining rooms,** 60 x 25 **feet, compels your admiration, by its elaborate magnificence. But what shall we say of the ladies' parlor, 100 feet long, by twenty feet wide ?—fitted with all modern acquisitions of hotel luxury. The sleeping apartments include 232 rooms, irrespective of private** *suites* **of chambers for the** *creme de la creme* **of society. You will be astonished when Mr. Swett tells you that this hotel requires the services of** 200 **employés during the summer season. Refreshed by our claret** we next drive to Trinity **Church, built on a rising** eminence, **and full of historic** interest in connection **with the** growth of the city of St. John. **The history** dates back to **1797.** That building on the other **side of the street,** a little **to the** south of where we are standing, **is the** scene of Manager E. A. **McDowell's many** triumphs. It is the Academy of Music, **not** **so large, certainly, but quite** as attractive as the Academy of Music at home. **Perhaps the decorations** of the former are **a** trifle too elaborate ; but its acoustic qualities are excellent. Now let us proceed to the Mechanics' Institute, **a plain, unpretentious looking building** on Carleton street, which has a history of its own **worthy of the progress** of this singular city. Of late years, the Mechanics' Institute has been **a** misnomer. You never see any mechanics there, and, so far **as** I **know, I** have never heard of its being patronized by artisans generally, except when the upper hall is let for popular entertainments. Suppose **we jump in our** vehicle once more and drive to the Young Men's **Christian Association** building on Charlotte street, a very neat edifice, **opposite the market house.** The rooms are comfortable and well furnished, **and are amply** provided with all that is attractive to young **men. But it is a query** to my mind whether **the Association is not somewhat of a failure from a socialistic standpoint. I have been there three times lately, and on any occasion I have never seen above half a dozen persons there. The supply of papers and magazines is not so large as might be wished. The hall, however, is very convenient and roomy, and is usually crowded when free meetings are held. Now let as drive to St. Paul's Church, Portland, which is undoubtedly, next to the Cathedral and Trinity** Church, the **prettiest and most tasteful church in the vicinity of St. John. It** has a good **choir, and an excellent organ, and** the general effect of the building on **a fine summer afternoon, when the sun is shining through** the stained glass windows, **is exceedingly handsome and impressive. Returning, suppose** we take the **Winter-street School-house, Portland, and glance at the** excellent **arrangements which are here provided for the instruction of the** " Blue-noses " **of the future. That they are good is but faint praise—they are more** than **good ; they are complete in every particular. Goodness is** only comparative, but the educational facilities which St. John and Port-land possess are superlative in their degree. The Victoria School-house, a handsome, new four-storey brick building, has accommodation for 1,000 children. It stands on the corner of Duke and Sydney streets, and is almost palatial in its proportions. Boston has nothing to equal it for similar purposes.

Now, let us pay the Jehu, and take dinner. What! two dollars for one hour's drive? Well, of course, we can't see the elephant for nothing, so we'll give you one and call it square.

MUNICIPAL.

St. John has an excellent fire department, poorly paid, and an inferior police force, which is paid quite as much as it is worth. The former deserves all that can be said about it in the way of praise. The men are quick and reliable, and their fire apparatus is in keeping with the excellent qualities of the firemen.

The police department is mixed. Its Chief is a hard-working official, who has on several occasions demonstrated that his special *forte* is his aptness for striking a "clue." During the past year he has had ample opportunities for the exercise of this important faculty; but, unfortunately, his subordinates lack the same perceptive power in following them up. Probably the St. John police force does not contain three men who may be termed professional policemen. They are poorly uniformed and disciplined, and have not arrived at that state of perfection you would expect to find in a city of so much importance. Seriously speaking, the St. John police force is fifty years behind the age. Every criminal here whose offence is above the grade of an ordinary "drunk" comes from Halifax—at least the papers say so, and, naturally, the case in Halifax is *vice versa*. But, unfortunately, recent experience has proved this rule does not always apply. Home criminals are occasionally discovered in their guilt, and accordingly punished. For such there is excellent accommodation in the city gaol, and not quite so good provision in the Provincial Penitentiary—a building respecting which the least said the better.

RAILROAD COMMUNICATION AND THE DEEP WATER TERMINUS.

St. John in a short time will be excellently provided for in this respect. The recent purchase by the Government of the Ballast wharf property at a cost of $40,000, for the purpose of a deep water terminus, has given general satisfaction. The intention is to run a short branch line from the Intercolonial at Marsh Bridge. This line is partially completed. The road will skirt Courtenay Bay, which extends from the Marsh Bridge, on the north-east side of the city, hugging the shore, and curving towards the south-west, and touching at Ballast wharf. The conditions under which the sale has been effected are that the Government will build the terminus 'or the receipt of grain and other shipments from all points of Canada; the city simply reserving the right of way for street purposes. The moving spirit in this purchase is said to be Mr. Bois de Veber, M P. The benefit is of course apparent, and there is no doubt that the work will be speedily pushed through.

By means of the Consolidated European and North American Railway from Bangor, St. John is reached.

The Grand Southern, now under construction, will be seventy-five miles long, and extend from St. Stephen, N. B., to Fairville, three miles from St. John. In all probability, the line will extend to the city.

I was almost forgetting to say something about

THE WATER AND GAS WORKS,

which are really a credit to the city, considering the miles of rock excavation which had to be blasted. These difficulties cannot be understood by those who have not visited St. John, and it is one of the crowning triumphs to the energy of the St. John people to say that in a short time every street in the city will be well supplied with water and gas. The Corporation deserves all the credit that can be given it in this particular.

JOURNALISTIC.

This letter would not be complete without some reference to the Fourth ~estate. St. John has five political papers—three dailies, one tri-weekly and one weekly. The *Daily Telegraph*, ostensibly a reform paper, is known throughout the Dominion for its enterprise and vigor. I hope I may be pardoned for intruding upon the " impersonality of journalism," as Mr. Goldwin Smith has it, in crediting those gentlemen connected with the press for their energy in making their journals what they have. W. Elder, Esq., M.P.P., editor and proprietor of the *Telegraph*, spares no expense in making his journal in every way worthy of its high reputation as a *newspaper*. He is an accomplished scholar and polished writer; a far-seeing politician, with an eye to the present and future requirements of the age. In making the *Telegraph* what it is, he has been ably assisted by Mr. James Hannay, sub-editor, a gentleman who has worked for, and knows more of the history and resources of New Brunswick than any one whom I have met. He has the history of St. John at his fingers' ends. He is not only a clever writer of great research, but also a poet of more than average ability. At present he has in the press a volume upon the "History of Acadia" of some five hundred pages. Mr. Hannay's services deserve recognition, and it is to him the St. John people are indebted for the vigorous fight the *Telegraph* made in defence of the Baie Verte Canal scheme. The *Evening Globe* is another spicy paper, partly owned by Mr. J. V. Ellis, recently appointed Postmaster here. The *Globe* is a reliable paper and you always know what it means, and it is credited with meaning just what it says. In popular parlance, you always know where to find it. The *News*, the avowed organ of the Orange party (also Reform), owned by Hon. E. Willis, is exceedingly popular with the Orangemen. Mr. J. L. Stewart is sub-editor, a pointed but somewhat reckless writer, whose ability is occasionally marred by sacrificing the truth for the sake of making a point. Mr. Stewart is a genial, well educated gentleman, possessing extensive information, combined with a shrewd, ready aptness for retort. Your correspondent trusts that he will not be massacred for speaking the truth. The *Freeman* (Roman Catholic, Reform) is owned by Mr. Anglin, Speaker of the House of Commons. Mr. Anglin is a hard foe to fight with on paper. His literary ability is unquestioned. A portly gentleman, courteous and conversational, he administers through his journal literary tonics to those of his contemporaries with whose opinions he may differ. His memory is wonderful, and it is currently stated that in past years he has printed reports solely from memory, without notes. He is a keen writer, unsparing in sarcasm, so roundly polished and carefully worded, that he is hard to beat in a fair, open field for discussion. The *Watchman*, owned by John Livingstone, Esq., the father of the Maritime Press, is a staunch Conservative weekly. He has already made his journal known far and wide for the series of very clever papers entitled, " Our Rulers in Council," the authorship of which is, so far, a mystery. Mr. Livingstone is a thorough journalist in the best sense of the word. He is comely in person, ready in conversation, and gentlemanly in tone. Where he gets his information whereon to base his papers referred to, nobody knows. The *Watchman* enjoys an extensive circulation, and its typographical appearance is second to no other journal in the Dominion. The staff of the *Watchman* has sustained a severe loss in the recent death of Mr. G. B. P. Fielding, of Cambridge University, a journalist formerly connected with the *Grip*, the *National*, and other Toronto papers. Your correspondent, who had the pleasure of his intimate confidence, can bear testimony to the excellent qualities of Mr. Fielding's head and heart—qualities which entitle him to the respectful admiration of every literary brother who knew him. Poor fellow! he now lies in the rural cemetery of St. John, with no stone to mark his grave—dead to the world's remembrances; but his loveable traits of disposition will ever live warm and bright in the hearts of those who recognized in him an ability far above the average of journalists. Had Mr. Fielding ever been permitted by health to live to the age usually allotted to mankind, he would have found his level and not have died in obscurity. For the sake of our profession, let us not permit his grave to remain neglected and unmarked. Mr. Geo. Stewart, Jr., also contributes to the *Watchman*. His name is well known as the former proprietor of. *Stewart's Quarterly*, a magazine which ought to have lived, but died for want of an educated public to appreciate its bright pages. No other magazine has yet compared with it for clever and sprightly reading. Mr. H. L. Spencer—a name well known to several Canadian journalists—also contributes to the *Watchman*. Mr. Spencer was formerly proprietor of the *Maritime Monthly*, which also came to its death from the same cause.

And now I must bring my letter to a close. I might tell you of the charming scenery about St. John; of the triumphs of the Paris crew; of its industries; of its fogs; of its 270,000 tons of shipping; of its lumber resources, but, alas, St. John and I must part company. Its people are warm-hearted, loyal and true British subjects, whose forefathers gave up all they had in defence of the British flag, and whose sons point with pride and reverence to the graveyard which contain the remains of the loyalist fathers. I might tell you with what pride they recount the history of the past; how their eyes kindle with kindly affection for our good Queen across the sea. I can only conclude by adding my humble testimony of their many sterling qualities; and as for their city, it will ever be kindly remembered by your correspondent, notwithstanding what Bayard Taylor and Charles Dudley Warner have written about it. And who shall say, with its railroad connections and winter harbor, that it possesses no interest to the good people of Montreal?

NO. XIII.

THE QUARRY AND MINERAL RESOURCES OF NEW BRUNSWICK.

One of the principal advantages which the Intercolonial Railway will be to New Brunswick is the assistance which it will give towards the development of the mineral wealth of the Province—more especially her granite, coal and plaster. The natural supply of these is unlimited. First in importance, let me tell you something about

THE RED GRANITE QUARRIES

which lie on the western shore of Lake Utopia. I reached them by stage from St. George, a distance of forty-seven miles from St. John, principally over rough road, but passing through a most delightful country. During my trip I had ample opportunity of witnessing the devastations made by the recent forest fires in the vicinity of Musquash, the smoke of which at times darkened the atmosphere by its density. These quarries are about two and a half miles from the town. The first and principal one is owned by the Bay of Fundy Red Granite Company; the second by the New Brunswick Granite Company, whose works are located at Carleton, opposite St. John. The quarries and land of

THE BAY OF FUNDY RED GRANITE COMPANY

comprise 1,320 acres. The ground is nearly all rock, and consists mostly of red granite ledges and hills, with a few spurs of ordinary trap rock, separated by narrow valleys of rich, loamy soil, through which numerous streams run, covered by beech, birch, pine, hemlock, spruce, and a little cedar. The timber varies from seven to fourteen inches in diameter.

The stone on the eastern and southern portions of the land is of a rich dark red color, with some ledges of a clear salmon color. Further west, and towards the northern boundaries of the land, the stone becomes lighter in shade.

In beauty of appearance, this latter shade is not to be compared with the deposits on the eastern, southern and southwestern portions of the land. The land known as the Gilmore or Ash lot is a perfect seam of ledges of a good color, with valleys between the ledges covered with a thick growth of fir and pine, with some small birch.

On the east side of the road there are a series of quarry faces of middling, good, and very good red granite; about two chains from the road and handy thereto. The stone here is in fine, large masses, most of it of very good quality.

The ledges run north and south nearly, but seem to radiate from a common centre, somewhere about the Gilmore or Ash lot, where they appear to concentrate.

It is utterly impossible to estimate the quantity of first-rate merchantable red granite contained within the limits of the Company's land. It is simply inexhaustible. There are hundreds of ledges, the outcrops of which represent from 5,000 tons to 100,000 tons each, while as to Gray's Mountain, which I estimate at 700 feet above the lake, being half a mile long and a quarter mile broad, and in Granite Mountain, estimated at 600 feet above the lake, one mile long and three-eighths of a mile wide. The granite on the land ceded to the Company is said to be perfectly free from those spots and veins which occasionally disfigure the Peterhead (Scotch) granite, and that, generally speaking, the ledges appear to be perfectly homogeneous or to lie in large rectangular slabs and blocks, generally inclined at an angle of about 30° from the north towards the horizon.

In only three instances, when making experimental blasts, (of which nearly one hundred have been put in), has seamy stone been met with.

Large deposits of good quartz sand, for grading purposes, extend along the beaches around the lake.

THE DISCOVERY OF THE GRANITE

was accidental. In the summer of 1872 Mr. C. Ward, Canadian artist of the *Illustrated London News*, at present Secretary for the Company, was desirous of fishing on Lake Eutopia. Mr. Ward approached a fisherman to hire his boat, which was anchored to the shore by a large red stone. In raising it, its rich color attracted his attention, and upon looking at it closely he once saw what it was, and it occurred to him it might be utilized for a better purpose than as a primitive anchor. Instead of going on his intended fishing excursion, he went hunting for red granite stone, and the result was the further discovery of immense ledges of beautiful, dark red granite—and the result is the existence of the present quarries.

But the beauty of the stone in its natural state is nothing compared to its richness when polished. To give you some idea of the vast proportions which this industry has assumed, let me say a word with regard to

THE POLISHING WORKS.

They are located on the Lower Falls, on the beautiful river of Magaguadavic, and within forty rods of the tide-water wharves. The power is obtained by a five-feet Lafelle (double turbine) wheel, with twenty four feet head. Its capacity is equal to one hundred and sixty horse-power. The foundations of the water-power machinery are laid in solid rock many feet below the river.

The buildings occupy three sides of a hollow square two hundred and eighty-four by one hundred and seventy-six feet. The enclosed yard is covered by a travelling crane, moving along as well as from one building to another. To this crane is attached a hoist of twenty feet, capable of lifting eight tons. The machinery consists in part of four carriages, running under vertical rubbers capable of polishing from seventy to eighty superficial feet; also four hand vertical machines, three double run of "pendulums," one lathe with twenty-eight feet by three feet swing, two of twenty feet by two feet; seven smaller lathes, besides iron and turning lathes, drill and wood lathe in the repair shops. There were in the yard when I was present two rough stones, for spires, twenty-two feet long by two feet six inches square at the base. At the quarry, there were two stones for columns, sixteen feet long by three feet six inches square. The men at that time were at work on an order for eighteen columns, thirteen feet six inches long and one foot nine inches and one foot ten inches in diameter. Four columns, weighing over ten tons each and three feet two inches in diameter, were sent to the Philadelphia public building last year. There are three decided tints of granite obtained from the quarries, but the bright, clear, red and light colored quartz predominate, and is generally preferred in the market. The lighter shades are so like the Scotch as to be scarcely distinguishable.

The works give employment to one hundred hands, the rate of wages ranging from 50 cents per day for boys, and $2.50 for the best stone-cutters. The best mechanics are Scotch.

The reputation which this justly celebrated granite has acheived may be inferred from the following facts and figures: Orders have been filled for Toronto, Galt, London, Guelph, Bowmanville, and Parliament Buildings, Ottawa, in Ontario; for the Lee Building, Boston· *Evening Post* Building, New York; Riviere Bank, Boston; New York Mutual Insurance Company's Building; Dime Savings Bank, New York; Public Building Philadelphia; Capitol Grounds, Washington; Baptist Church, Chicago; Central Park Bridge; San Francisco; Florida; St. John Post Office, and various other places in New Brunswick. These and smaller orders represent nearly $80,000, and yet this important industry is still a puny infant compared with what it doubtless will be in the future. The quarries of

THE NEW BRUNSWICK RED GRANITE COMPANY

are about two miles from the former, and though occupying a less extensive area the nature of the granite remains mnch about the same. The polishing works have recently been removed to St. John. It is needless to recapitulate a necessarily similar description of these works. There should, and probably will be, sufficient capital to carry on a highly renumerative business for both companies. The quarries of this Company are silent at present, although some thirty hands were busily employed when I was in St. John. The transportation of this granite over the Intercolonial *via* the

GRAND SOUTHERN RAILROAD.

will be greatly facilitated when the latter road is completed. It will be from seventy-five to eighty miles in length, with it termini at St. Stephen, N. B., and St. John. The Provincial Government has given a subsidy of $5,000 per mile. It will be a narrow gauge (three and a half feet) and will connect at Bangor, thus making the line from Bangor to St. John forty miles shorter than at present. J. N. Greene, Esq., of New York, is the contractor, and when I tell you some twenty miles of road have been graded in two months, you will have some idea of its rapidity of construction. The maximum grade is seventy-nine feet per mile. The sharpest curvature is a 717-feet radius. The road bed seems to be built in a solid, substantial manner. There are no wooden structures, the culverts being all of granite. The principal difficulties will be the bridging of the Digdewash and Magaguadavic, also at Popologan, Little Big, New Rivers and Musquash. The latter will be a draw bridge. It will probably be completed next fall. The advantages are that the Grand Southern will materially shorten the route to Prince Edward Island, Halifax, St. John and Bangor. The nature of the soil through which the line passes is loam and gravel, with a small portion of clay. I drove over about nine miles of it and so far as I could judge the work was well done. Next in importance are

THE ALBERT MINES

near Dorchester. These were also discovered by accident in 1850. Some consider it a variety of jet, others think it a coal, while some suppose it to be asphaltum. The vein has a thickness of from one inch to seventeen feet, and it has been excavated to a depth of 1,162 feet. Since its first discovery the following shipments have been made :—

```
1863.........................................18,600 tons.
1864..........................................19,300
1865..........................................20,500
1866..........................................20,500
1867..........................................17,000
1868..........................................12,400
1869..........................................17,000
1870.......................................... 6,000
1871.......................................... 5,500
1872.......................................... 5,000
1873.......................................... 6,000
1874.......................................... 7,000
                                              ---------
     Total.................................154,800 tons.
```

The Government royalty since Jan. 1st, 1866, amounts to $8,029.29 The albertite has been and is extensively used in the manufacture of oil and for mixing with other coals in the preparation of gas. It will yield 100 gallons of crude oil or 14,500 cubic feet of gas per ton, leaving, when used with other coal, a valuable quality of coke. It has been sold for from $15 to $20 per ton. The mines give employment to about 100 men.

In the vicinity of Dorchester, at Budreau village, are several

FREESTONE QUARRIES.

The most important is owned by the Caledonia Freestone Company. This excellent stone for building purposes was first quarried in 1856 from the Budreau property, since which time the annual shipments have averaged from 5,000 to 7,000 tons. The Caledonia quarries were opened in 1864. The company ships annually between 5,000 and 6,000 tons. There is also another quarry at Mary's Point, Hopewell, and a third at Shepody Mount, Albert County. These stones are remarkable for their color, durability, and the ease with which they may be cut. They are almost free from pyrites. The beds now being worked vary from two to six feet in thickness. Blocks thirty feet long, weighing thirty tons, can readily be obtained.

In the same county, at Hillsboro, a few miles from Dorchester, you strike the

GYPSUM DEPOSITS

of the Albert Manufacturing Company. This mineral is distributed in irregular masses with sandstone, marls and limestone. The richness of the gypsum deposits is without limit. A portion of the rock now being worked, from ninety to one hundred feet, contains a thickness of seventy feet of pure gypsum, resting on beds of plaster of unknown depth. In its neighborhood are large masses of snow-white alabaster, exceedingly beautiful. There are extensive works erected here for grinding and calcination, which have been in almost continuous operation since 1861. An average of 600 barrels per day can be worked up, giving employment to about 100 hands.

The following statement for 1875 will give you an idea of the scale which this industry has achieved at Hillsboro :—

Plaster quarried, in tons, ... 129,000
Do.   shipped in rock, in tons...................... 5,500
Do.   ground and calcined, in barrels................ 47,200
Do.   do.   for farming........................... 800

The present price of the crude and ground plaster is 65c. per barrel, duty free ; calcined, $1. This, however, is subject to a duty in the United States of twenty per cent.

Gypsum is also found in large quantities at Petitcodiac (delivered at the station of the Intercolonial Railway for 70c. per barrel, or 40c. in bulk) and at Tobique River, Victoria County. The railway will doubtless develope the facilities for manufacturing and shipping this valuable mineral.

As it would be impossible to do justice to the natural resources of New Brunswick in less than a month, I have condensed the remaining portion of the subject matter of my letter from a handy little pamphlet entitled "The Woods and Minerals of New Brunswick," written by Prof. L. W. Bailey, of New Brunswick University, and Edward Jack, Esq , C.E., Surveyor of Crown Lands. (The collection of woods sent to the Centennial Exhibition from this Province contains over seventy distinct specimens, which are too numerous to even mention casually in a single letter.)

IRON.

The reader may have noticed that the arrangement of the minerals in this letter is irregular. The fact is unavoidable, for the reason that those previously noted are within easy distance of each other and are directly connected with the Intercolonial Railway for shipment. The railway would be of little use did it not affect more or less the growth of the mineral wealth of the Province, and it is in order to make it more readily known that I have now referred to it in this concluding letter upon New Brunswick.

Bog iron ore, or liminite, is found in Burton, Sunbury County, and in the parish of Maryland, in York County. Queen's County also contains it to some extent. It extends over considerable areas, and has attained in some instances a thickness of four or five feet, but no attempt has yet been made to smelt these ores. A recent analysis of a specimen from Sunbury County gave forty-seven per cent. of metal.

RED HEMATITE

is found at Jacksontown, near Woodstock, two miles from the west bank of the St. John River, Carleton County. The ore was first discovered by a geological surveying party from Maine, in 1836, under Dr. Chas. T Jackson, who traced it from the Aristook region north-eastward to the St. John River, and to the eastward of the latter, in bands extending fifteen or twenty miles in length, over the north and north-eastern portions of the county of Carleton. The width of the ore beds is from six inches to eight feet, the average thickness being three and a half feet.

Forty thousand tons have been smelted at the Woodstock works while in operation, and the metal is remarkable for its admirable adaptation to the manufacture of steel. It also contains a large percentage of manganese.

COPPER.

This valuable mineral is found at Salmon River, Albert County ; Adams Island, Charlotte County, and at Grand Manan Island. It is mostly found in connection with a band of rocks extending along the southern coast of the Province. These ores have not been worked, although several attempts have been made. This is owing to the fact that they have not yet been ascertained to be sufficiently concentrated to pay the cost of extraction. A specimen from Salmon River is said to have yielded sixty-two per cent. of copper.

At La Tête there is a large tract of copper. A shaft is being sunk to a depth of 25 feet, on a lode about four thick. Another shaft is being sunk two hundred feet from the former where good indications have been found. The cost of labour being low, these mines, it is thought, would be highly remunerative. From samples of copper already submitted, their richness is beyond question.

MANGANESE.

Deposits of black Oxide of Manganese, associated with more or less of manganite, have been mined at Quaco, Markhamville, Kings County, and at Shepody Mountain. The mineral is chiefly met with in connection with limestones lying near the base of the series, distributed in the form of veins, but chiefly in irregular masses, some of which are exceedingly pure. The mines at Markhamville were first opened in 1863, since which time 6,000 tons have been mined. The annual yield varies from 500 to 1,500 tons. The mines are eleven miles from the railway and the ore is subject to a cartage of $3 per ton, but nevertheless they have been profitably worked. The price varies from $15 to $50 per ton. Manganese is also met with near Bathurst and in Kings County. The existence of

ANTIMONY

although known for a number of years, attracted little attention until 1862, when fresh discoveries were made, and several companies were formed in the parish of Prince William, York county. The mineral extends over an area of several square miles, occurring chiefly in white quartz veins, with intersections of hard clay slates and sandstones. The veins vary in thickness from a few inches to six feet. A great deal of ore has been obtained within a short distance of the surface by means of trenches dug on the course

of the lodes ; but shafts have been sunk to the depth of something over
100 feet. Extensive works have been erected on the property of the Lake
George Mining Company, including an 80-horse power engine, a 30-horse
power air-compresser engine, a Burleigh steam drill, Blake's crusher rollers,
and other apparatus for desulpherization and smelting. When in full operation fifteen tons of metal were obtained every six weeks ; the charges
(of 500 cwt.) yielding from forth-five to fifiy-five per cent. of regulus, The
fluxes used are charcoal, soda, or salt cake, and rosin. The value of the
metal on the ground is twelve to fourteen cents per pound. It is exported
to the United States and is valued in Boston at $12.25 to $12.75, gold, per
ton. It is also used at the works in the manufacture of Babbit metal (containing fifteen to twenty per cent of antimony, with lead and tin, or in the
better qualities, with lead, copper and tin,) and valued at from 20 to 50
cents per pound.

BITUMINOUS COAL.

The only locality in which mining operations for this mineral are conducted, is in and about the Newcastle river and along the shores of the
Grand Lake, in Queen's county It is estimated that more then one-third
of the Province is occupied by rocks of the coal formation. The seam of
Grand Lake, a thickness of 22 to 26 inches, is sufficiently great to be
capable of working. The seams are usually nearly or quite horizontal ;
they cover considerable areas, and when sufficiently near the surface are
readly removed. The beds near Newcastle River and Grand Lake are about
two feet thick, and are usually met with within 10 or 15 feet of the surface.
Coal has been removed from a number of points covering an area of over
one hundred square miles, indicating a total production capacity of nearly
155,000,000 tons. The mineral is a true bituminious coal of the caking
variety, and is employed for household and blacksmith's use. The
total annual production is about 2,000 chaldrons, which is sold in St. John
from $4.50 to $8.00 per chaldron.

BITUMINOUS SHALE.

These shales are principally found in the vicinity of the Albert mines, of
which they form the enclosing rocks. They extend to the eastward and
westward of that locality for over fifty miles. The shales are tough, dense
and fine grained, and, when rubbed, of a strongly bituminous odor. Several
fruitless attempts have been made at various times to use these shales in
the manafacture of oils, and works were erected at Baltimore, a few miles
distant ; but operations were abandoned owing to the heavy import duties
imposed by the United States, as well as to the heavy competition with
natural oils in that country. The shales in the best bed at Baltimore yielded 63 gallons per ton, and were capable of yielding 7,500feet of gas per ton.
In 1865 about 2,000 tons were received from similer beds in Westmoreland
county, and sold in the United States at the rate of $6 per ton.

It is somewhat singular that the New Brunswick press has been hitherto reticent in the matter of the natural wealth of its Province. But it is an encouraging sign to note the exertions (notwithstanding the depression which in the freight business is said to have touched bottom) which are being made to bring these industries into public notice by the formation of public companies and in other ways. Capital is not wanted ; but the chief requisite so far seems to have been the want of experienced men who thoroughly understand the capabilities of the various rescources at their disposal. Before closing let me say I have just heard that a rich vein of anthracite coal was discovered a few days ago at Little Lepreaux, on Mace's Bay, near Lepreaux Harbor. The news has caused some excitement, but is belived to be true.

No. XIV.

HALIFAX, N.S.

Halifax, whose history dates back from July, 1749, like that of its sister city, St. John, is full of interesting associations, not necessary to repeat here. They form a part of the history of the Dominion, and the more important facts are familiar to almost every school boy. But the Halifax of to-day has an attraction to the tourist which cannot be overlooked. Its beautiful situation, its magnificent harbor, its splendid scenery, its military connections, its ocean traffic and its splendid buildings cannot be described in detail in a single letter. The front of the city fringes the well sheltered harbor, and as you turn towards the south and east from the citadel the panoramic stretch of scenery gradually melts into the purple haze of horizon and golden light. The picturesque abounds everywhere. Indeed, you may look from almost any point and you will find something new to charm you, whether it be hill, river, island or lake ; or with a good field glass you may take in one of the sublimest views the most enthusiastic admirer of Nature could desire.

The excellent shelter afforded by MacNab's Island, which lies at its mouth, gives security to the shipping from wind or tempest. The island is thickly covered with hardwood, and in the full beauty of its summer foliage it can scarcely be surpassed for pictorial effect. Eastern Passage lies to the east of the island, while to the western extremity of the island, on Meagher's Beach, stands the lighthouse.

St. George's Island, which literally lies in the heart of the harbor, protects it from invasion from hostile foes. The island is oval, and is strongly fortified with several large guns, which command the city, wharves and shipping.

The appearance of the city from the citadel is a peculiar mixture of spires, smoke, house-tops and dust: and perhaps it cannot be truthfully said that, so far as the city itself is concerned, the view from this point does it justice. The northern part of the city, or " North End," as it is called, is conspicuous for its many beautiful private residences. To the west is " Dutch Village," while to the southwest of the town we reach the head of the Northwest Arm, dotted with islands. Along the " Arm " several fine mansions and country seats are being erected in the centre of rich woodland, and the white houses present a very charming effect of light and shade. Following the same direction the Park is reached, situated in the centre of all that is lovely to the eye. West of the citadel lies the Common, where "field days" are held by the garrison troops. South of the Common are the Public Gardens, containing about twenty acres. They are really a credit to the city, and are equal to anything of the kind I have seen in the Dominion. West of the Public Gardens you have Camp Hill Cemetery, somewhat unattractive in its silent gloom

The city has a population of about 30,000 souls. It is three miles long and about one mile wide.

PUBLIC BUILDINGS.

The Post Office building in Hollis street may be said to be in the business centre of the city. Close by are the Parliament buildings in Hollis street, and near them is the Young Men's Christian Association building, a four-storey edifice, recently erected, which is quite as imposing in its exterior proportions as the one in Montreal. On the opposite side of the way is the new Masonic Hall, on Pleasant street, and St. Mary's Cathedral, and also close to it is the Government House.

The Halifax Club on Hollis street is also a modern handsome edifice, from the centre of which the social phase of Halifax society may be said to graduate. In addition to the numerous commercial and banking institutions, many of which are fine noble blocks of solid stone, Halifax has reason to be proud of its

FREE PUBLIC LIBRARY,

which contains some 10,000 volumes, and is free to all who wish to read them. Naturally enough, the citizens pride themselves upon having an institution in their midst which is so well conducted as this appears to be.

EDUCATIONAL AND CHARITABLE INSTITUTIONS.

For its size, Halifax has more charitable institutions than any other city in the Maritime Provinces. Including the Asylum for the Insane at Dartmouth, opposite the city, erected on Mount Hope, and the Inebriate Asylum near First Lake, there are no less than fifteen benevolent institutions for " all sorts and conditions of persons," where the blind, the maimed and the halt can receive gratuitous assistance. To detail these as they deserve would require a special article. These societies, both religious and secular, are a credit to the city and to the persons who personally interest hemselves in their development. The asylums for the insane, and for the blind and deaf and dumb, deserve especial mention.

THE FORTIFICATIONS

attract a large number of tourists, who throng the various forts and keep the military officials busily engaged in replying to an endless number of questions. At the present time it is estimated there are about 2,000 troops in the garrison, consisting of the 60th Royal Rifles, the 87th Foot, the Royal Horse Artillery, and some detachments of the Corps of Engineers. The soldiers have every facility for enjoyment and mental improvement. Libraries, reading-rooms, billiards, refreshment rooms, where a good cup of coffee and bread and butter may be had for three cents, and, in fact, everything a man can reasonably want may be obtained. The opinion, however, was frequently expressed to your correspondent that the present term of enlistment (six years) has failed to answer the purpose originally intended. The friends of the measure supposed that a better class of men could be obtained, but experience has proved, by the sample of recruits sent out from England since the new Enlistment Act has been in force, that the very opposite has been the result. The physical and moral status of the soldier of to-day is much inferior to that of ten years ago. Old and well-tried men are fast leaving the service, and the result is the introduction of an element entirely at variance with the requirements of a good soldier.

Just now there are no ships of war at the station, and the only vessel of interest at present laying up is the Faraday, belonging to the Atlantic Cable Company—one of the most complete scientific vessels afloat. It is fitted with every improvement known to electricians, and it has on more than one occasion demonstrated its fitness for the service of repairing Atlantic cables.

THE CITADEL,

or, as it is known, the "Star Fort," is to an inexperienced eye the perfection of military construction. But, strange to say, recent events have proved it is far from being as strong as was formerly supposed. This is illustrated by the fact that at the time of my visit the engineers were repairing some twenty feet of wall, four to six feet in thickness, which had given way from the shock caused by the firing of the morning and evening gun! A recent writer in *Vanity Fair* has well said, in speaking of the Royal Engineers, that they have been principally engaged of late years in repairing each others' work. This is strictly true, as may be seen by the recent improvements in several of the forts along the harbor, which were necessitated by the mounting of eighteen-pounder guns, to accommodate which extensive alterations had to be made in the original plans of some of the fortifications, which had only just been completed when the guns arrived from England. If Halifax people had to pay for these enormous renovations it would soon become a bankrupt city.

Two miles from the centre of the city is Fort Ogilvie, and near it Fort Cambridge. These forts are, of course, made as strongly as military science can make them. They are built of granite. Close to the shore are Point Pleasant Battery, the Northwest Arm Battery, and, upon the summit of the Park, the Prince of Wales' Tower. These are old fortifications, and are supposed to be retained "merely for the look of the thing." Not far from the Northwest Arm is Melville Island, now a military prison, formerly used as a place of confinement for the prisoners captured during the war of 1812-14. St. George's Island stands in the centre of the harbor, and contains one of the strongest, if not *the* strongest of forts. Fort Charlotte, lately rebuilt, is considered as strong as modern science can make it. On the eastern shore of the harbor is another formidable structure named Fort Clarence. Another line of batteries on the northwestern shore of McNab's Island commands the harbor below St. George's Island. In addition to these are the martello towers on Meagher's Beach and Sambro Island, while on the land side is York Redoubt. Halifax harbor may be truthfully said to be the Cronstadt of America. The military cemetery is at Fort Massey, near the south end of Queen street.

COMMERCIAL.

Halifax is the terminus of nine lines of steamers, also the terminus of the eastern division of the Intercolonial Railway, as well as the starting point of the Windsor & Annapolis Railway. Recently an effort has been made to resuscitate a Chamber of Commerce; but it is an extraordinary fact that nothwithstanding the vast amount of capital, the natural wealth of mines within its reach, and the immense advantages which its beautiful harbor possesses for winter trade, the commercial enterprise in Halifax is nominally dead. Let me give you an illustration. Not long since, a meeting of citzens was held to organize a Board of Trade. Speeches were made subscriptions were promised, and all the enthusiam created by a "novelty" was brought to bear upon the subject. But, unfortunately, the first spasm of interest was also its last, and to-day the Halifax Board of Trade meets in a dingy, badly lighted room where it would be difficult to crowd fifty persons into it without making everybody feel uncomfortable. This fact seems to be significant of the people. There can be no doubt about the matter, that in point of superiority Halifax harbor is far ahead of St John. It is comparatively free from tides, and not liable to dense fogs to which sailors are subjected in approaching St. John harbor. But on the other hand the merchants of St. John do business, probably, with half the Province of Nova Scotia. There is no want of capital, but there is a large deficiency of pluck and energy which contribute to the vitality of a people.

SOCIALISTIC.

Society in Halifax is largely imitative. It patterns itself after the fashion of the military. If the military aristocracy of the Halifax Club say "so and so is the correct thing," society in Halifax follows suit and asks no questions. Whether this is a good or a bad sign, it is not for me to say; but it would certainly appear that unless any special affair is "under the patronage of the officers of the garrison," Halifax proper holds aloof and becomes cold and unsympathetic. The consequnce is that the really intellectual portion of society keeps within doors and shuts itself up within the limits of its own circle, while the superficial and "swell" element delights in driving tandem and making itself generally obtrusive and remarkable. The hospitality of the garrison is unquestionable, but it is somewhat trying to one not initiated into the mystery of military life to hear people going into rhapsodies about Captain Smith's "dawg" or "Major Jones's" jolly thing in horseflesh; or, it may be, "Lieutenant Black's love affair with Mrs. Somebody-else, awfully rich, you know." Of course fashionable society everywhere possesses more or less shallowness; but in Halifax it is very hollow, and the echo is proportionately large.

THE PRESS.

There are five daily papers published in the city, the oldest of which is the *Acadian Recorder*, established in 1813. The more influential morning papers are the *Herald* and the *Chronicle*; the former is in the Conservative and the latter in the Reform interest. The evening papers are the *Citizen* and the *Reporter*. In addition to these there are several weekly secular and religious journals. The daily papers, however, are creditable to the city, but could be made more so if there was sufficient enterprise in the city, out of which good material for journalistic ability might be made. As it is, this want, at times, is very much felt, and helps to retard the progress of journalism. From a purely literary standpoint there is much ability in Halifax, but it is somewhat cramped because at times there is really nothing to write about. A good hotel is sadly needed in the city. True, there are the "Halifax" and the "International," where strangers receive every attention; but the city is growing, and year by year it is thronged with tourists. There can be no doubt that, in this respect, Halifax can learn something from St. John. In conclusion, the future of Halifax is largely in the hands of its people, who, so far as my exerience goes, are exceedingly kind and hospitable. Naturally, it is surrounded by everything that is beautiful. Not only is it particularly favoured in a picturesque sense, but its environs contain large mineral deposits, of which more will be said in a future letter.

XV.

THE ANNAPOLIS VALLEY.

Leaving the Intercolonial at Halifax we take the train of the Windsor & Annapolis Railway *en route* for Annapolis, passing through one of the most beautiful stretches of scenery to be found on the continent.

From Halifax to Windsor, forty-five miles, the road, which is now in capital condition, runs through a country of rocks and hills. At first the surroundings do not impress you with any special admiration until you reach Bedford Basin, a beautiful sheet of water, around which the railroad runs for a distance of eight miles.

At the head of the Basin is the village of Bedford, famous for its shad fishing. Leaving it we pass through miles of forest scenery full of interest from its imposing character.

The next place worthy of notice is Windsor. Here the River Avon is spanned by an iron lattice girder bridge 1,160 feet long, supported on piers and abutments of free stone. It was erected at a cost of £32,000. The town, which is famous as the seat of King's College, the oldest university in the Province, is built on a large hill, and overlooks one of the most beautiful views it is possible to imagine. The far-famed Basin of Minas, with Cape Blomidon in the distance, reminds us that we have just entered

"THE LAND OF EVANGELINE,"

celebrated in Longfellow's immortal poem. Miles of orchard gardens, where trees are loaded down with golden-colored, rich, juicy-looking fruit, gives one an impression not soon forgotten. The sweet-scented hay perfumes the atmosphere with its grateful fragrance, and instinctively we recall the lines:—

> " In the Acadian land, on the shores of the Basin of Minas,
> Distant, secluded, still, the little village of Grand Pré
> Lay in the valley."

The Grand Pré of to-day, however, is in direct contrast with the poetical description given by Longfellow, for the inhabitants appear to be the most common-place of mortals. It is difficult to imagine that Longfellow has never visited this spot, but has written solely from imagination. Again are we reminded of the beauty of his description as we leave Grand Pré :—

> "Still stands the forest primeval; but under the shade of its branches
> Dwells another race, with other customs and language.
> Only along the shores of the mournful and misty Atlantic
> Linger a few Acadian peasants, whose fathers from exile
> Wandered back to their native land to die in its bosom.
> In the fisherman's cot the wheel and the loom are still busy;
> Maidens still wear their Norman caps and their kirtles of homespun,
> And by the evening fire repeat Evangeline's story;
> While from its rocky caverns, the deep-voiced neighboring ocean
> Speaks, and in accents disconsolate answers to the wail of the forest."

Close by the stations of Grand Pré, tradition says there is an apple tree under which ashes have been found, and where "Basil's forge" is supposed to have been located. But it strikes me this is a flimsy attempt to palm off some spurious legend upon the traveller. Whether or not it follows that a forge should have been located at this particular spot merely because ashes were found there I cannot say, but as nobody can prove that Basil did *not* erect a forge there, let the tradition pass without further comment.

But permit me to give you a legend of probably a more truthful character. It consists of a copy of

A LETTER FROM THE POET,

received by Mr. J. P. Edwards, a conductor on the Windsor & Annapolis Railway, and which will explain itself :—

[Copy.]

CAMBRIDGE, Sept. 25, 1875.

MY DEAR SIR :

I have had the pleasure of receiving from Mr. Hemmell the two canes which you were kind enough to send me as a *souvenir* of Acadia, and hasten to thank you for this mark of your regard.

It has never been my good fortune to see the beautiful country through which you pass daily, and I fear I shall never see it—save in imagination. All the more shall I prize the branch of the apple tree from Grand Pré and the white ash cane from the top of Bloomidale.

I beg you to accept my cordial thanks for your kindness in sending them, and to believe me,

Yours very truly,

HENRY W. LONGFELLOW.

We next reach Wolfville, which boasts of a college of some repute, situated in the midst of a thriving and industrious community. Some of the most conspicuous features of the country through which we pass in this section are the huge dykes, comprising hundreds of acres, reclaimed and protected from the Bay of Fundy by the original settlers, Acadian French. These dykes enclose some of the richest hay grounds in the Province.

KENTVILLE

is the next place of importance. Here are the head offices of the Windsor & Annapolis Railway. The rural beauty of the place strongly reminds one of some lovely garden spot in Kent or Devonshire. The air is pure, the scenery is beautiful, and the people are clean-looking and happy. The air is particularly pure and refreshing, and indeed this charming spot is unsurpassed for its many natural beauties. The village lies in a valley bounded by the Cornwallis River, and is contiguous to the far-famed " Garden of Nova Scotia," in which it should be included as a part. The vicinity is not only blessed by its rich crops of fruit and natural situation but excellent salmon and trout fishing may be had during the season. Woodcock, snipe, partridge and duck are to be found in abundance during the autumn, when hundreds of tourists pay their annual visit.

A short distance from Kentville we enter the great apple-growing country of the Dominion, which lies in

THE ANNAPOLIS VALLEY,

rich in everthing that is charming to the eye. The fertility almost exceeds belief, while the beautiful landscapes along its border delights the eyes and refreshes the senses, the mountains in the distance making a bold back-ground pleasant in its relief and grandeur.

After casually noting Berwick, Aylsford and Kingston, the next stopping place of any importance is

MIDDLETON,

chiefly remarkable for the falls on the Nictaux River, and the iron mines. The scenery in the vicinity of the North Mountains is said to be extremely fine.

Passing Lawrencetown, we next arrive at

PARADISE.

Whoever named this place Paradise, is either the prince of satirists or the simplest of humans. Paradise, as seen from the station, is not a lovely view, but as seen from a distance it may in all sincerity be said that

"Distance lends enchantment to the view,"

so far as Paradise is concerned. The place is as great a misnomer as Paris in Vermont. Indeed I half suspect that some jealous American had something to do with originating the Paradise of Nova Scotia, and the reason why I think so is based upon the following story, which is vouched to me as being correct. (By the way, there's always a certain amount of risk in relating another person's "original" story.) However, here it is :—It is said that a Nova Scotian, upon asking an ancient Vermont farmer who it was who named one of the stations along the line of the Vermont Central Railway, Paris, was told that it was called after Jeremiah Paris, who formerly owned the land on which the station was built.

"Then its origin has nothing to do with a young lady by the name of Helen?" remarked the enquirer.

"If yer mean Helen Bigelow, maybe it has," cos I believe one of the Parises married a Bigelow gal."

"Then probably the person I mean might have been a relation, a third cousin perhaps. The lady I refer to was Helen o'Troy."

The farmer "'lowed he didn't know any such person, leastwise not in his time."

Crossing the Annapolis River, the road from Bridgetown, the next station, to

ANNAPOLIS ROYAL,

runs through the same charming country in the midst of a rich valley.

Annapolis stands on the first site of the first town settled in Acadia. Originally the town was named, by De Monts, in 1605, Port Royal.

Ferland (cours du historie du Canada) says :

"Port Royal, now Annapolis, founded in 1605, is the first durable settlement formed by the French in North America, and the most ancient town in this part of the world after St. Augustine." Annapolis, in all the old records, bears a conspicuous part as being the headquarters of the French in the New World. It has stood siege after siege, and attacks from all quarters.

Portions of the old fortifications are still standing, while from the summit a glorious prospect of the surrounding country may be seen.

For thirty-six years Annapolis was the seat of Government, when in 1749 it was transferred to Halifax. On the opposite side of the river is Granville, a place of some note in connection with shipbuilding.

And now I must close my brief description of this beautiful tract of country, and acknowledge the courtesy of the kindly officials of the Windsor & Annapolis Railway for the facilities they have extended your correspondent in writing up the natural garden of Nova Scotia.

The Company has provided easy and comfortable coaches, and notwithstanding the huge difficulties with which it has had to contend in the past, the excellent road-bed, and the charming scenery through which the road runs, will doubtless secure in the future a large amount of traffic from the neighbouring Province and the United States. The fishing and shooting, in its proper season, is good, and so far I could observe there is ample hotel accommodation along the road.

No. XVI.

THE MINING INDUSTRIES OF NOVA SCOTIA.

The extensive area in Nova Scotia covered by its mineral deposits is so vast as to render the difficulty of preventing even a general idea of the subject very great.

A personal inspection of these large tracts of coal, iron and gold has rather the effects of bewildering the tourist than of adding to his stock of information in regard to them. It is, therefore, the intention of your correspondent to give as far as available the results, from the best authorities, of their workings.

COAL.

The Report of the Department of Mines for the year 1875 is very conci
upon the subject, and from it we take the main facts in this article, having
reference only to the large and more important workings.

CUMBERLAND COUNTY.

The trade of Cumberland County alone shows an increase; exceeding
by 11,000 tons that of the previous year. The increase steadily rose from
14,000 in 1872, to 26,000 in 1873; and from 49,600 in 1874, to 60,944 tons
in 1875. The local sales were 1,000 tons of round and 1,000 of stock, in
excess of the year before; and the exports of New Brunswick increased
11,000 tons; while the trade with the United States decreased 2,000 tons.
These figures are given in round numbers.

JOGGINS COAL MINES.

On lease 31, adjoining, on the south, that of the Joggins Coal Mining
Association, a bore-hole was put down at the corner where the road turns
in to the Joggins Mine, and the Joggins Main Seam pierced at the depth
of 1,028 feet. The hole was made by an American diamond drill, owned
by Mr. John Logan and others, of Pictou—the same that was mentioned in
in the last Report as having done its work so well.

No other reports of explorations made in this field have been received
except from the New Dominion Coal Company, who have further proved
the seams on the area of the Hon. A J. Smith The level on the main
seam has been driven 400 feet, and from it two drifts have been driven
northerly, which have intersected two other seams; the first two feet three
inches thick, at a distance of sixteen feet, and the second twenty-two
inches in thickness, at a distance of twenty-nine feet from the main seam.
It is expected that a slope will be put down on the main seam during the
summer, to test the quality of the coal to the deep. The seam varies in
thickness from four feet to five feet six inches, with a parting of fire clay,
which, under more of the cover of the hill, is only six to eight inches in
thickness.

CHARACTER OF THE MINE.

Professor J. W. Dawson, F. G S., remarks in his work entitled "Acadian
Geology," 1858, pages 189, 190 191 :

" Coal.—Only one deposit of this mineral in now worked in Cumberland.
The Joggins Main Seam, consisting of two beds, three feet six inches and
one foot six inches thick, with a clay parting between, varying from one
foot to a few inches. It is a free burning bituminous coal of a fair quality.'

The specimen of Joggins coal from Main Seam is bright coal of uniform texture, with straight joints containing fibres of iron pyrites and calcareous matter.

Moisture	2·5
Volatile Combustible Matter	36·3
Fixed Carbon	56·0
Reddish Gray Ashes	5·2
	100

In further confirmation of the good character of this coal, it may be said a very large number of certificates received from practical, reliable men who have used it for steam and manufacturing purposes, and who testify cheerfully to its superior steam-producing quality, its cheapness compared with other coals, and also to the very encouraging fact of its gradual and continued improvement as greater depth is obtained; and so far as the science of geology can determine, the quantity of coal contained in this seam is considered unlimited.

SPRING HILL.

The mining of coal from the West or Hall Slope has been stopped, the workings alone being kept free from water. In the East or Byers Slope the levels have been so extended that the faces are now 800 feet apart.

The level going east has met with some difficulties, being first troubled with a roll in the floor, and then with a thickening of the parting. The rooms have been driven horizontally twelve feet wide, leaving pillars seven or eight yards in thickness. One counter-balance has been put up on the east side, and two on the west, to lower the coal from the upper rooms to the level. The workings are drained by a direct acting steam pump which forces the water a vertical height of 427 feet, through a column 820 feet long. The pump has a twenty-two inch cylinder, thirty inch stroke, and nine inch plunger. To clean the slack coal of dust and fire clay, and to prepare it the better for market, a screening apparatus has been erected.

The coal from the screen is hoisted by a small engine forty-two feet above the track, and passed through a circular screen four feet in diameter and twenty-two feet long. The upper nine feet is of five-eighths-inch mesh; then follows four feet of half-inch mesh, and then nine feet of seven-eighths-inch mesh. The coal that passed through the upper lengths is thrown away, and that which goes through the lower is called nut coal.

The fine coal which is thrown away, possibly might, if it were washed, make good coke in a proper oven. The rough experiment noticed under the head of COKE cannot be accepted as a final test of the value of this coal for coke; and as there is every likelihood of the demand at Londonderry being large, a proper trial should be made.

PICTOU COUNTY.

The total coal sales of this county, while they exceeded those of 1873 by 3,000 tons, show a decline, when compared with the trade of the year before, of nearly 21,000 tons—a quantity which is less by some 20,000 tons than that of the sales of the Acadia Company are short of their annual average. That company has again yielded the first place in the list of shipments, which for some years it held, and the Albion Mines have regained their old supremacy. The falling off in the home consumption is small—4,000 out of 107,000 tons; in the United States trade it is very considerable, over 29,000 tons; and in the trade with the West Indies nearly 17,000 tons. These heavy losses of trade were in part balanced by the considerable increase in the shipments to the Province of Quebec, 32,000 tons more than the 116,000 sent in 1874. The trade with other markets showed fluctuations of little moment. There is one increase yet to be noticed, that in the demand for slack, which has steadily advanced Prince Edward Island being the largest customer, and taking 26,000 tons.

ALBION MINES.

The pair of stone drifts from the main seam in the Foord Pit have reached the deep seam, at a distance of 185 yards, and proved it there to contain twenty feet of good coal. The stone parting, which is four feet thick to the rise, was found only nine inches thick, and the overlaying coal to have increased from four feet to four feet six inches in thickness. This satisfactory condition of the seam has induced the starting of an incline, from the Cage Pit workings, in a south-easterly direction, to open up that portion of the deep seam. Until the drifts from the main seam proved the coal to be of good quality, doubts had been entertained, because of the inferior quality of that immediately to the rise, into which, some time ago, levels had been driven. The principal operations in the Cage Pit have been towards the north, and three counter-balances are now going on that side of the incline, and one has been started off the level on the south side. The under-ground engine has been replaced by another which brings the rake up with greater ease and speed. The return air-ways have been enlarged, and some 30,000 feet of air now circulate through the workings. The special pump at the foot of the incline now delivers the exhaust steam into the suction, and while freeing the workings of a great inconvenience assists the pump at its work, The boilers on the surface have been shedded over, whereby a saving of fuel is effected, and protection given to the stokers during inclement weather. The great distance to which the steam has to be taken underground causes a condensation of over 50 per cent., and doubtless a saving would be effected were the steam pipe coated for its entire length with some non-conducting material.

In the Foord Pit the north levels have, for some time, been checked by a fault which has at last been pierced, and the coal found beyond. The south side also met a fault, but which was not expected to give much trouble.

In hoisting the coal, the double-deck cages holding four tubs are now used, and thus about 80 per cent. more coal can be brought to bank in a given time.

For the workmen, additional accomodation of a superior class has been provided. A boarding house containing fourteen rooms, and eight blocks of two dwellings, each having a porch and containing two rooms.

VALE.

Some changes have been made in the method of working the McBain Seam at this colliery. The pillars are now twenty feet thick, and the bords have been widened to sixteen feet. A second level has been driven below the main level as an air and water course, and horses have been introduced to facilitate the transit. On the west side a fault of twenty feet has been met with and pierced.

On the surface there are now ninety-two tenements for the accomodation of the workmen. Near the junction with the Pictou Branch Railway a locomotive shed has been put up, and a new locomotive obtained, suitable for the ordinary guage to which the railway track was changed during the summer.

No work of any moment was done on Mitchell and Barton's area.

CAPE BRETON COUNTY

The continued decline in the production of coal in this county has been a source of much suffering to the mining population, and it is greatly to be feared that unless a change for the better soon takes place in the trade, numbers of the men usually employed about the mines will have to seek elsewhere for work and in new occupations find employment. For not even in the United States are the collieries open to them, since the trade is there equally as dull and overdone as it is here.

Comparing the past with the previous year, there appears a total decline of 32,314 tons; made up principally in the reduced shipments to the United States and West Indies, to which countries, dull as the trade was during the preceding year, nearly 18,000 and 15,000 tons were then sent. The home consumption merely shows an increase of three hundred tons. The trade with Newfoundland shows alone a marked increase, some 5,000 tons. This advance, however, can hardly be considered permanent, as the supplies were unusually short in St. Johns during the winter of 1874-75, and those held in the present winter of 1875-76 are unusually large.

In addition to the foregoing, large tracts of coal are being worked more or less in Victoria, Inverness, and Colchester counties, but the Report does not give any financial statements concerning them.

COAL ANALYSES.

SEAMS.	Specific Gravity.	Moisture and Volatile Matter.	Fixed Carbon.	Ash.	Sulphur.	Coke in Lbs. per Ton.	Cubic Feet of Gas per Ton.	Candle Power.	C. ft. Gas purif'd by 1 bar. Lime.	AUTHORITIES.
Joggins (Main).......		38.80	56.00	5.20						Dawson.
Victoria	1.34	36.00	51.84	12.16			9,340			
Spring Hill (13 feet seam)		25.38	60.95	13.67						How.
				10.80	.84					Woodhouse.
		35.39	60.46	4.15	.22					Hartley.
Black Seam, 11 ft.		31.08	64.94	3.98	.51					Dr. Percy.
				5.05	1.09					
	1.32	29.63	56.98	13.39	.77		7,180	15		Johnson.
Albion (Main)		29.53	60.83	9.62						Dawson.
	1.30	25.75	66.50	7.74	.55					How.
Albion (Deep)	1.33	26.74	61.65	10.25	.89					Broome.
	1.34	23.00	68.50	8.50	1.68					How.
McGregor	1.32	22.90	67.85	9.35		1640	9,500	13		Manhattan Gas.
Stellar	1.10	66.56	25.23	8.21	.00					How.
	1.32	34.37	57.57	7.55	.50					Broome.
Acadia	1.31	29.93	60.35	9.46	.26					Broome.
	1.32	31.69	60.32	7.56	.42					Broome.
McBain	1.36	25.45	62.63	11.92	.49					How.
Collins.	1.27	36.75	57.10	6.06						Chapman.
		38.80	55.80	5.40						Dr. Torrey.
Blockhouse		40.80	55.70	3.50		1460	10,217	17	2304	Manhattan Gas.
		31.94	62.79	5.25	3.75					Harrington..
Phelan	1.32	37.26	58.39	4.35	2.17		9,500	16.5		
		35.47	61.67	2.86	2.06					Harrington.
Emery...........		38.10	58.45	3.45			9,500			Percy.
		31.75	66.85	1.40	1.21					Harrington.
Lorway (Gardiner)..		34.33	61.97	3.70	1.18					Harrington.
Hub		36.54	62.53	.93		1484	9,560	13	1945	
		28.62	65.85	3.24	2.29	1342	10,080	16		Harrington.
	1.27	36.28	58.56	5.16		1480	9,844	16.7	1850	
		30.21	67.78	2.01	.90					Harrington.
Harbor..		38.50	56.50	5.00						Manhattan Gas.
		34.09	62.92	2.99	2.29	1440	10,106	17	2314	Harrington.
	1.28			7.81	2.18	1441	9,900	17		Imperial Gas.
Lingan...........		35.20	60.80	4.09		1450	9,520	13	2200	Chandler.
		34.23	63.98	1.79	.77					Harrington.
		30.03	66.91	3.06						How.
Ross		38.70	58.40	2.96						Dawson.
	1.33	26.94	67.57	5.49						Johnson.
Sydney (Main).		31.87	64.59	3.54			6,500			How.
	1.30	34.18	61.50	4.32	1.24					How.
Edward's	1.27	36.74	56.97	6.27						Chapman.
	1.53	28.88	60.45	7.25	3.42					
McAuley		36.15	58.01	5.70	2.34	1510	9,000	15		Richard.
		32.07	64.43	3.50	2.86					Harrington.

For other analyses see How's "Mineralogy of Nova Scotia, 1868," and the Geological Survey Reports of Progress.

THE NOVA SCOTIA COAL TRADE WITH THE UNITED STATES AND ELSEWHERE.

There is one feature of the general trade which, as it shows a healthy condition, is well worthy of more than passing attention—it is the trade with the neighboring Provinces. Even in competition with free American coal, it has more than doubled within the last four years.

Coal sold to neighboring Provinces :

1871	168,577 tons.
1872	285,433 "
1873	337,993 "
1874	338,754 "
1875	381,711 "

| | Nova Scotia Sold | | Canada Imported From | |
	At Home.	To other B. N. A. Provinces.	United States.	Great Britain.
1871..	150,232	168,577	216,633	190,680
1872..	199,886	285,433	....	177,904
1873..	215,295	337,983	428,455	131,338
1874..	214,965	338,754	671,224	186,753
1875..	212,630	381,711	512,835	....

| | Nova Scotia Exported to the United States. | | | Canada Imported from the United States. |
Years.	Quantities.	Duty.	Authority.	
1865....	465,194	Free.	United States.	
1866....	404,252	$1.25	Custom House.	
1867....	338,492	1.25	Reports.	
1868....	228,132	1.25	"	
1869....	257,485	1.25	"	
1870....	168,180	1.25	"	216,633
1871....	165,431	1.25	"	
1872....	154,094	1.75	"	428,455
1873....	264,760	1.75	Nova Scotia Dept. of	
1874..,.	138,335	1.75	Mines Reports.	671,124
1875....	89,746	1.75	"	512,835

THE GAS COALS EXPORTED WERE SENT FROM THE FOLLOWING CAPE BRETON PORTS.

Ports.		To New York.	To New England.
Cow Bay,	about	10,899 tons.	458 tons.
Sydney,	"	11,172	870
Caledonia,	"	445	7,584
Glace Bay,	"	1,941	914
Lingan,	"	760	13,786

IRON.

The importations by the Dominion of Canada during the fiscal year ending June 30th, 1875, of pig iron, amounted to the value of $1.229,989, and of railway bars, fish plates, &c., to the value of $5,289,454.

The Londonderry Mines, which are controlled by the Steel Company of Canada, it is thought, will be the means of developing the inexhaustible quantity of ore which lies beneath the surface. The extensive preparations which were being made at the time of my visit, were of a character which is extremely creditable to the Province. The two blast furnaces alone, it is expected, will produce 600 to 700 tons of metal per week. The amount of pig iron, however, consumed by the Lower Provinces does not exceed 600 tons annually, and consequently a market will have to be sought in Ontario and Quebec. The mining department is under the charge of Capt. Bryant, an experienced and able English miner, who has under his charge some 300 miners, of whom a large number are Cornishmen.

Some 16 adits have been driven at the principal points along the line of the deposits. At Cook's Brook one has been driven to the west 580 feet, and it has yet to go 350 feet before it is expected to cut the ore bed at a depth of 150 feet from the surface. Another has been driven in the east bank 585 feet, and has yet to go 230 feet more to reach the deposit of the ore. At Slack's Brook an adit has been driven 980 feet, and it is shortly expected to strike the ore. A surface level, No. 2, at Martin's Brook, proved the existence of much ore in ground supposed to be nearly worked out. No. 7, the lowest adit of all, has been driven 1,290 feet. On he east side of Londonderry the mining operations have been confined to Folly Mountains, where five adits are in course of being driven at various depths, for draining the extensive ore deposits already discovered in that locality. The deepest striking the ore ground 250 feet from the surface. The total quantity of ore in sight is variously estimated up to 300,000 tons.

To convey the ore from the West Mines at Martin's Brook to the furnaces at Londonderry, a tramway of three feet guage, and two and a half miles long, has been built and laid with steel rails; and a branch of the ordinary four feet eight inches and a half guage, five **miles long, connects the East Mines,** at the base of Folly Mountain, with the **Intercolonial Railway a** DeBert Station, and so with the **works** at Londonderry.

There are also some good **iron ores** at Cleveland, **on the west side of the Nictaux** River, **Annapolis County, which are** said **to be of good quality.** At Springville, **on the east river of Pictou, extensive iron deposits exist.**

The following **Statement shews the quantity and value of Pig Iron** imported **into the Dominion of Canada by Provinces during the three** months **ended 30th September, 1875.**

PROVINCES.	Cwt.	$	REMARKS.
Ontario	49,957	47,520	Hamilton principally.
Quebec	221,980	176,812	Montreal and Quebec only.
Nova Scotia	3,340	2,671	Halifax principally.
New Brunswick	11,700	9,692	St. John only.
Manitoba	11,700	9,692	
British Columbia	11,700	9,692	
Prince Edward Island .	502	408	Charlottetown.

LEAD.

This mineral is found near Port Hood, Guysborough County, C.B. The out-crop is said to be, at the latter place, from eight to fifteen inches wide, and to contain bands of pure galena from two to three inches wide. An analysis recently submitted gave 86·12 of lead and ·44 of silver, or an equivalent of 15·75 ounces per ton.

COPPER

has been found near Polson's Lake, Antigonish County. A vein was found by sinking to a depth of sixteen feet to the bed rocks, over which a drift was driven that laid bare the vein. An analysis made by Prof. How gave 19·21 of metalic ore, and another sample 29·7 of copper.

GOLD.

The general opinion existing among bankers in Halifax with reference to the gold yield of the Province is that, if the mining is carried on with discretion and if owners are satisfied with a fair per centage of profit upon their capital, there is no reason why it cannot be worked profitably. But so far, "sensational" experiments have hitherto proved a failure, and have given the various claims a fictitious value during the temporary excitement.

Mr. A. Heatherington, F.G.S., states the gross yield of gold from the

rarious districts of Nova Scotia, from 1861 to 1875 inclusive, to be as
follows :

DISTRICT AND PERIOD.	GROSS YIELD.		
	TOTAL QUANTITY		VALUE. At $19 46·6 Canada Currency per oz.
	ozs.	dwt. gr	$ c.
Sherbrooke............................	73,966	4 6	1,439,875 60
Waverley............................	49,875	14 7	970,913 90
Renfrew	27,060	4 5	526,772 08
Wine Harbor........................	24,367	9 15	474,353 63
Montagu............................	15,806	17 21	307,707 53
Oldham............................	15,785	12 3	307,293 13
Tangier............................	12,593	8 13	245,152 05
Stormont	10,996	0 11	214,055 92
Uniacke	8,261	11 15	160,825 45
Caribou	3,162	3 6	61,556 76
Ovens....	2,292	8 6	44.625 64
Unclassified........................	1,890	8 16	36,800 48
Gay's River........................	1,472	11 3	28,765 75
Lawrencetown	542	0 15	10,551 54
Total................	248,072	14 22	4,829,149 46

It may be mentioned that an excellent vein has been found at Fifteen
Mile Stream, near New Glasgow, which has been partly developed by Mr.
James Jackson.

In conclusion your corrrespondent would remark that with proper enterprise and activity, with that practical knowledge necessary to the development of the enormous natural wealth possessed by Nova Scotia, there is
no reason to believe but what she has a powerful agent in the Intercolonial
Railway ; but so long as the means of their realization is wanting ; so long
as her capitalists remain inactive, so long will these hidden treasures of
the earth remain comparatively useless.

www.ingramcontent.com/pod-product-compliance
Lightning Source LLC
Chambersburg PA
CBHW020257090426
42735CB00009B/1113